MIRIAM MATHEW

When Nothing Is Wrong

(But Everything Feels Off)

First published by Miriam Mathew 2026

First edition

ISBN: 978-1-9194417-1-9

For those who noticed the shift before it had a name.

For those who were told nothing was wrong,
and learned to trust what their body already knew.

For those who stayed kind without becoming compliant,
and left without needing permission.

This book is for you.

Power is most effective when it does not announce itself.

Miriam Mathew

Contents

Author's Note

This book was not written to persuade you.

It was written to name what many people experience but struggle to explain: the moment your inner life begins to withdraw before anything is openly wrong. The moment you can still list reasons to stay, but your body has already stopped consenting.

I am not interested in diagnosing people. I am interested in documenting patterns—the quiet mechanics of power in intimate relationships: how control reveals itself through tone, timing, structure, and inevitability; how "reasonable" arrangements can be designed to immobilise; how fairness can provoke hostility; how silence can function as a strategy.

This is not a book about men. It is a book about power and perception. You do not need to have been abused to recognise what follows. Many readers will find themselves here long before harm ever becomes visible. Others will recognise the sequence in hindsight and understand why clarity arrived when it did.

Either way, the aim is the same: *to restore your trust in your own perception*—without drama, without shame, and without requiring you to prove what you already know.

How to Read This Book

Read this slowly.

Not because it is difficult, but because it is diagnostic. Many of these pages will not feel like "new information." They will feel like language finally attaching itself to something you have already lived.

This work is not a call to expose, confront, explain, or fix anyone. It does not ask you to diagnose others, justify anger, or act before you are ready. What it offers is *internal clarity*—not instruction, not urgency, not performance.

How you move, if you move at all, is contextual. Sometimes the safest clarity is invisible.

A few guidelines will help:

Do not force certainty. This book is built for the space before certainty—the interval where something feels off, but evidence is incomplete.

Treat your reactions as data. If a passage makes your chest tighten, if you feel sudden fatigue, if your mind wants to argue or explain—note that. The body registers power shifts with precision.

Do not read it as a checklist. This is not a set of rules for identifying "bad people." Patterns are not proofs. Patterns are signals—especially when they repeat.

Do not read it to fix someone. If you approach these pages searching for the right words to make another person become mutual, you will miss the point. This book is not for converting control into partnership. It is for recognising when a partnership is not what is being offered.

Let silence do some of the work. Some chapters end without "what to do next." That is intentional. Clarity does not need theatrics. It needs space.

If clarity brings discomfort, pause. You are not required to act, explain, disclose, or decide anything in real time. *Recognition does not obligate response.*

If you recognise yourself in these pages, the goal is not to alarm you. The goal is accuracy.

This is not an action guide. It is a *map of recognition.*

A Note to the Reader

This book is written from a particular relational frame, and it may help to name it before you begin—not as a defence, not as a manifesto, but as an act of precision. What follows is not a universal claim about all relationships, cultures, or belief systems; it is a specific lens, used deliberately, to examine how power, care, and humanity are organised between people.

Throughout these pages, the word ***equality*** is used in a specific and limited sense. It does not refer to sameness, identical roles, or interchangeable strengths. It refers to something more foundational: **equal humanity, equal moral worth, and equal entitlement to agency**. It names the baseline beneath difference, not an erasure of difference itself.

This book assumes that no person's value exceeds another's, and that no relationship is healthy if one person's inner life, dignity, or autonomy must shrink to keep the connection intact. Any bond that requires self-reduction as a condition of continuation is not examined here as intimacy, but as structure.

Men and women are not identical. People differ in temperament, capacity, history, and strength. But **difference is not hierarchy**. **Variation is not permission**. And love does not require one person to become structurally smaller so another can feel secure. Distinction does not justify dominance; complementarity does not excuse erasure.

Some readers find the language of equality confronting—not because it denies difference, but because it removes moral justification for domination, entitlement, or unreciprocated endurance. It destabilises narratives that rely on one person bearing disproportionate costs while calling that arrangement a virtue. This book does not argue politics or theology. It examines **relational structure**—what happens repeatedly and predictably when power is unevenly distributed.

When equality is referenced here, it refers to **mutuality**: shared risk, shared responsibility, shared dignity. It refers to relationships where both people are permitted to remain whole—where neither person's humanity must be managed, contained, or subordinated for the bond to survive.

If you hold strong personal, cultural, or religious values, this book does not ask you to abandon them. It asks only that **goodness not be confused with submission**, **faith not be used to silence discernment**, and **love not be defined by who absorbs the most harm**. Values are not weakened by clarity; they are clarified by it.

You are not required to agree with every premise to read this book well. But understanding the frame it is written from will help you recognise what is being named—and what is not. It will help you distinguish between a critique of structure and a critique of belief, between an examination of power and a judgement of personhood.

With that orientation, you may begin.

Introduction

When Nothing Is Wrong (But Everything Feels Off)

Nothing was wrong.

There was no crisis you could present as evidence. No clear betrayal. No single moment that would earn unanimous agreement. If you tried to explain it, you would sound vague. If you insisted on it, you would be told to relax.

And yet, something had shifted.

Not loudly. Quietly.

It is difficult to describe the earliest stage of danger because it does not feel like danger. It feels like misalignment. Like a small internal withdrawal. Like the loss of a particular kind of openness. You still show up. You still try. You still give the benefit of the doubt. But something in you stops leaning forward.

Fear is urgent and loud. Discernment is quiet and exact.

This is the stage most people ignore.

Because we have been trained to recognise harm only when it becomes undeniable, we are taught to wait for proof. To be fair. To be patient. To explain things away. To look for a more generous interpretation.

But the body does not wait for proof. It registers a pattern.

The body notices when questions are met with deflection instead of engagement. It notices when fairness is reframed as conflict. It notices when a partner becomes more invested in winning than understanding. It notices when the tone changes while the words stay polite. It notices when "structure" appears where care should have been.

The mind often comes later. The mind wants a story. The mind wants certainty. The mind wants a clear villain, an apparent reason, a precise moment.

But most coercive dynamics do not begin with cruelty. They start with positioning.

A person moves closer, not to build mutuality, but to secure access. The relationship becomes less about connection and more about terms. Not stated at first—implied, tested, introduced gradually and normalised by repetition.

And because it happens quietly, the person experiencing it often doubts herself.

She asks herself whether she is being too sensitive. Whether the past is contaminating the present. Whether she is asking for too much. Whether she is failing at love by refusing to relax.

This book is for that moment.

This book begins before the confrontation. Before ultimatums. Before collapse.

It begins at the moment your body knows something your life has not yet had to answer for.

It does not exist to inflame you. It exists to clarify you.

It is not interested in labelling people. It is interested in naming the mechanics that turn intimacy into leverage and partnership into hierarchy.

If you are reading this because something feels off—even though you cannot yet prove it—this book will not ask you to be louder. It will not tell you to be nicer. It will not instruct you to wait until your discomfort becomes an emergency.

It will do something quieter and more useful:
It will give language to what you already know.

When Questions Change the Atmosphere

Negotiation is often misunderstood.

In healthy relationships, negotiation is a sign of mutuality: two people aligning their lives with honesty, care, and shared responsibility. It is a mechanism of partnership.

But in control-based dynamics, negotiation serves a different function.

It does not lead to agreement. It reveals the architecture.

The moment you begin negotiating fairness—real fairness, not performative compromise—you start touching the part of the system that cannot survive. You are no longer discussing preferences. You are challenging the arrangement's organising principle.

And that is why, in certain relationships, the tone changes as soon as you ask a reasonable question.

The question may be simple:
What happens if one of us becomes unwell?
How will assets be structured?
How do we ensure both parties are protected?
What does marriage mean to you in practice?
What is expected of me—specifically?

The content of the question is not the provocation.
The provocation is your insistence on mutuality.

Because mutuality introduces constraints: limits, accountability, exposure, shared risk.

In control-based systems, the goal is not a shared life.
The goal is secured advantage.

And secured advantage depends on asymmetry.

This is why negotiation often triggers escalation.

Not because you asked wrongly.
Because you asked at all.

When a person is offering a partnership, they can tolerate questions. They may feel discomfort, but they remain oriented toward understanding. They can explain, adjust, and collaborate without punishing the conversation.

When a person is offering control disguised as commitment, negotiation threatens the disguise.

Fair questions do not invite more clarity.
They invite pressure.

Pressure may arrive as: **moral language** (*"that's what marriage is"*); **spiritual framing** (*"yield or submit"*); **character attacks** (*"you're showing your true colours"*); **false ultimatums** (*"if you can't accept this, stay single"*); **contempt disguised as counsel** (*"don't marry—you're* *independent")*; **withdrawal** (*"I'll call you later"*); **dismissal** (*"you've said what you said"*).

It may also arrive more quietly—and therefore more effectively—as: **urgency** (*"we need to decide now"*); **practical framing** (*"this is just how things work"*); **financial pressure** (*"this is the sensible option"*); **logistical inevitability** (*"it's already in motion"*); **social comparison** (*"everyone else manages this"*); **pathologising concern** (*"are you anxious?"*); **tone policing** (*"you'd be heard if you said it differently"*); **future-faking** (*"it will be better once we're married/settled / secure"*); **gratitude pressure** (*"after everything I've done"*); **responsibility shifting** (*"you're making this difficult"*); **reasonableness theatre** (*"let's be rational"*); **silence used as consequence**; **affection made conditional**; **competence flattery** (*"you're the strong one—you can handle this"*).

These pressures do not seek understanding.
They seek compliance.

Notice what all of these have in common:
they do not answer the question.
They control the asker.

Negotiation, in these dynamics, is treated as rebellion because it exposes a truth the system depends on keeping hidden:
That your agency still exists.

When Being Seen as Human Is Treated as Disrespect

Many people enter these relationships believing something fundamental: that they are already recognised as fully human.

They assume that respect, consideration, and reciprocity are the baseline — not rewards to be earned, but the minimum conditions of intimacy. They believe that if they provide care, empathy, patience, and understanding, those qualities will be reciprocated. That humanity will be met with humanity.

What they do not realise — until much later — is that this assumption was never shared.

In control-based dynamics, the victim is not encountered as a full peer. They are encountered as *less than*, or as instrumental: valuable for what they provide, regulate, absorb, or stabilise — but not entitled to the same moral consideration as the person exerting control.

This is why the moment the victim asks to be treated as fully human often produces shock.

They are not asking for dominance.
They are not asking for an advantage.
They are asking for recognition.

And that request is experienced as disrespect.

Not because it is unreasonable, but because it violates the hierarchy upon which the relationship is built.

To someone who has unconsciously positioned themselves as superior, equal treatment feels like insubordination. Mutuality feels like loss. Fairness feels like theft. And being asked to consider another person's reality feels like an offence against their rightful authority.

This is why victims are often stunned by the reaction.

They thought they were negotiating terms.
They were actually challenging status.

They believed they were asking to be seen.
They were revealing that they had never been.

And once that realisation lands, it reframes everything that came before:

- Why negotiation escalated instead of resolved
- Why clarity provoked punishment
- Why fairness was met with rage
- Why dignity was treated as defiance

The problem was never *how* they asked.
It was that, in this system, they were never meant to ask at all.

A control-based partner does not fear your anger as much as he fears your clarity. Anger can be framed as an indicator of emotional instability. It can be used to discredit you. It can be baited and managed.

But clarity is different.
Clarity does not argue.
It observes.
It names.

And naming collapses the fantasy that the system is mutual.

This is why many people feel a deep internal shift during negotiation.

Not panic. Not hysteria. A quiet recognition that cannot be undone.

They realise:
If fairness must be punished, the relationship is not safe.
If questions are treated as disrespectful, a partnership is not being offered.
If mutual protection is framed as greed, love is being used as a mask.
If the arrangement requires your silence to function, it was never designed for your flourishing.

And the pattern sharpens:

If clarity is met with hostility rather than dialogue, the system depends on confusion.
If negotiation triggers threats, withdrawal, or contempt, consent was never real.
If your needs are recast as attacks, the relationship survives only by your self-erasure.
If accountability is experienced as betrayal, power—not intimacy—is being protected.
If your growth destabilises the bond, the bond was built on your diminishment.
If peace is offered only in exchange for compliance, safety is conditional.
If you must manage another person's emotions to remain protected, you are not in partnership—you are in containment.
If the cost of honesty is punishment, the truth was never welcome there.

This is the moment the body often goes first.

It stops leaning forward. It becomes less persuasive. It begins preparing for exit before the mind has finished gathering reasons. This is not dramatic. It is sober. It is the nervous system recognising that the environment is no longer reciprocal.

Negotiation becomes the final warning because it shows you what happens when you try to bring reality into the relationship.

In a relationship grounded in mutuality, reality is welcomed.
In a relationship grounded in control, reality is treated as a threat.

And once you see which one you are in, you cannot unsee it.

Negotiation, then, is not the beginning of repair.

It is often the moment the arrangement reveals itself.
Not because you failed to communicate.

But because you finally spoke to the structure instead of the story.
And structures answer with force when they cannot answer with truth.

I

✦ THE BODY KNOWS FIRST ✦

Perception before explanation

This part begins before language.
Before evidence. Before anything, you can easily explain.
It begins in the body—where safety, power,
and threat are registered long before the mind assembles meaning.

These chapters trace how discomfort, intuition, calm unease,

and discernment arise early, quietly, and accurately.
Not as fear, but as perception—often overridden, rarely honoured,
and almost always right.

✦ Discomfort Precedes Evidence ✦

Why the body registers power shifts early • Why "unease" is not anxiety • The intelligence of quiet withdrawal

Discomfort rarely arrives with an explanation. It does not announce itself with logic or arrive carrying evidence neatly arranged for review. It arrives before language. It arrives before permission. It arrives as a change in posture—inside you. A subtle loss of ease. A tightening you cannot justify. A hesitation that does not come from fear, but from accuracy. A knowing that does not argue. A pause that does not need consensus.

This is the body registering something the mind has not yet been allowed to name. It is perception without narrative. Information without justification. It is the nervous system noticing shift, incongruence, misalignment—often long before the intellect is permitted to catch up.

Most people are taught to distrust this. They are trained early to override it, to interrogate it into silence. They call it overthinking. They call it baggage. They call it anxiety. They pathologise what cannot yet be explained. They are rewarded for ignoring it, praised for being "easy", "flexible", and "reasonable". They learn that certainty must be rationalised to be valid—and so they learn to wait until harm is undeniable before they listen.

But discomfort is often the first honest signal in the room. Not because you are fragile—because your body is paying attention. Because it is tracking tone before words, pattern before promise, cost before consequence. Because it has learned—through repetition, through exposure, through survival—that what feels slightly wrong early often becomes unbearable later.

Discomfort is not panic. It is not imagination. It is not a weakness. It is the body's refusal to pretend neutrality when something is already leaning out of alignment. It is intelligence operating beneath politeness. It is truth arriving before it is welcome.

And the more you honour it, the less it needs to shout.

1. Why the Body Registers Power Shifts Early

The body is not philosophical. It does not negotiate meaning. It does not ask whether something is reasonable, forgivable, or well-intended. It does not wait for permission, proof, or consensus. It notices what the mind can still excuse. It responds to reality before interpretation, to consequence before justification, to power before narrative.

Before you have a story, you have a sensation. Before you can articulate concern, your body has already adjusted its posture towards the situation. It registers tone before content, timing before intention, atmosphere before meaning. It knows when you are being met—and when you are being managed. It does not require clarity to react; it reacts because clarity has not yet been allowed.

A person can say the right words while their body communicates something else entirely: impatience masked as efficiency, contempt softened by politeness, ownership framed as care, control disguised as concern. The mind listens for sentences. The body listens for safety. The mind is persuaded by explanation. The body responds to exposure.

And safety is not merely the absence of threat. Safety is the presence of mutuality. Safety is not calm achieved through compliance; it is steadiness sustained through shared power.

Mutuality has a feeling. It is not abstract. It is somatic. It feels like being able to ask a question without consequence. It feels like your reality can enter the room without being corrected or punished. It feels like your no does not become an argument. It feels like your needs do not become evidence against your character. It feels like difference does not trigger discipline.

When mutuality begins to erode, the body notices first—not dramatically, not hysterically, but consistently, not through alarm, but through adjustment. You may not be able to name a single incident, yet something in you starts to shift. You explain more than you should. You leave conversations feeling subtly diminished. You rehearse sentences before speaking. You anticipate defensiveness. You begin monitoring the other person's mood as a strategy for peace. Your nervous system quietly reallocates energy from expression to management.

Nothing is overtly "wrong". Nothing is loud enough to point to. Nothing violates a rule that could be cited cleanly. And yet something essential is no longer free. Something once implicit—your right to exist without calculation—has become conditional.

This is the earliest stage of coercion—not violence, not chaos, not cruelty—but repositioning. A quiet redistribution of power that does not announce itself as harm. It arrives politely. It sounds reasonable. It presents as normal. And because it does not look like danger, it is often overlooked.

Who gets to define reality? Who gets to end conversations? Who gets to be complex while the other must stay simple? Who gets to be tired while the other must remain steady? Who gets to be human—and who must be careful.

The body reads these shifts because it lives inside consequences. The body is where consequence lands. The mind can hold hope, context, and the benefit of the doubt. The body holds a pattern. And pattern is how power is felt long before it is understood.

2. Why "Unease" Is Not Anxiety

Anxiety is loud. It surges, spirals, and demands resolution. It multiplies possibilities and searches frantically for certainty. Anxiety pulls attention forward, outward, everywhere at once.

Unease moves in the opposite direction. Unease is quiet. It does not escalate—it withdraws. It does not speculate. It recognises. Unease does not ask, *What if something goes wrong?* Unease says, *something already is.*

An anxious system is flooded. **An uneasy one is precise.**

An anxious person often feels unsteady in many places. Unease is specific. It does not scatter across life indiscriminately; it concentrates. It gathers itself around one relationship, one environment, one repeating interaction. It localises where power, safety, or freedom are beginning to distort.

Anxiety tries to resolve. **Unease tries to protect.**

This is why unease is so often misunderstood. It does not look like a crisis. It does not collapse functioning. It does not announce itself as distress. It looks like a person becoming slightly less available—less eager, less persuadable, less willing to move forward without clarity.

It looks like a woman who can still laugh, still perform competence, still meet expectations—while something inside her quietly stops leaning in.

And because the withdrawal is calm, it is treated as irrational. She is told to relax. To stop analysing. To trust more. To be generous. To give it time. To not "ruin something good".

But unease is not asking to be soothed. **Unease signals that soothing will not resolve what is being registered.**

Unease arises when reassurance conflicts with trajectory—when words promise safety but structure quietly removes it. It is the nervous system detecting incongruence between what is being said and what is being built.

This is why unease can exist in relationships that are polite, well-intentioned, and free of overt cruelty because unease does not measure niceness.

It measures direction.

Unease is not concerned with whether something is tolerable today. It is concerned with what continuation will require tomorrow. The body does not only ask, *Is this safe now?* It asks, *What will this demand of me if it continues?*—and it often answers long before the mind is ready to listen.

Unease is not anxiety in disguise. **It is discernment before language.**

3. The Intelligence of Quiet Withdrawal

Quiet withdrawal is not weakness. It is discernment acting without permission.

It is the body reducing exposure because it has learned something the mind has not yet named.

Withdrawal begins in small ways: you stop volunteering as much; you stop offering your inner life freely; you stop sharing plans that can be used against you; you stop seeking comfort from the person who causes the discomfort; you begin conserving yourself.

People misunderstand this because they equate love with openness. But openness is not a virtue in unsafe systems. **It is a resource.**

In healthy relationships, openness deepens intimacy. In control-based dynamics, openness becomes leverage.

Your vulnerabilities become tools.
Your history becomes a map.

Your generosity becomes a channel.
Your patience becomes permission.

Quiet withdrawal is the body protecting what it can still protect.

This is why some people react badly to it. They do not ask, *Are you okay?* They ask, *What's wrong with you?* They do not ask, *What changed?* They accuse: *You're changing.*

They do not become curious. **They become controlling.**

Because withdrawal removes what they were using: *access.*

To a mutual partner, your withdrawal is concerning. To a controlling partner, your withdrawal is insubordination.

And here is the brutal truth: *if your calm withdrawal provokes punishment—if your hesitation is met with pressure—if your caution is reframed as character failure—your body was not overreacting.*

It was observing.

Quiet withdrawal is often the first boundary a person sets before they are ready to set one out loud. It is the nervous system saying, "*I will not offer more of myself to a structure that does not protect me.*"

Discomfort Is Not the Enemy

Many people treat discomfort as something to overcome—as a flaw, an obstacle to love, a sign of immaturity. It is framed as something to outgrow, override, rationalise away. Something to manage quietly so the connection can be preserved and harmony maintained. In this framing, discomfort becomes a personal failing rather than a source of information.

But discomfort is often the first evidence you receive—not evidence of wrongdoing, but evidence of misalignment. Evidence that something subtle has shifted beneath the surface. Evidence that what once felt reciprocal is beginning to tilt. Evidence that what was once mutual may now be conditional.

Evidence that something is being tested. Evidence that your reality is becoming inconvenient. Evidence that the relationship may require you to become smaller to continue. Not smaller because you are wrong—but smaller because expansion would disrupt an emerging imbalance.

This is why discomfort so often arrives before explanation. Before proof. Before language. The body does not wait for clarity; it responds to pressure. It responds to the early redistribution of power—when access begins to outpace care, when closeness starts to require self-editing, when your presence is welcomed only if it remains manageable.

This chapter is not teaching you to be suspicious. **It is restoring precision.** It is not asking you to doubt people; it is asking you to trust what you register. It is not inviting fear; it is returning authority to perception.

Because when your body begins to withdraw, it is rarely random. Withdrawal is not always avoidance. Sometimes it is recognition. Sometimes it is the earliest form of self-respect—your system adjusting before your mind has caught up.

Discomfort precedes evidence because power shifts before it speaks. Control rarely announces itself. It reorganises quietly. It changes tone, timing, and consequence before it ever changes language. And the body, attuned to consequence rather than story, responds first.

And once you learn to respect that signal, you stop needing a disaster to justify your boundaries. You stop waiting for harm to become obvious before you honour what you already know. You no longer require betrayal, cruelty, or collapse as permission to protect yourself.

You begin earlier.

Where freedom actually begins.

✦ Intuition Is Not Fear ✦

How fear is loud and fast · How discernment is calm and steady · Why people confuse the two

Intuition is often dismissed because it is mistaken for fear.

And fear has earned its reputation. Fear can be irrational. Fear can be loud. Fear can turn one ambiguous moment into a disaster narrative. Fear can make you reach for certainty at any cost—texts, explanations, reassurance, resolution.

But **discernment is not fear**.

Discernment is not panic. It is not suspicion. It is not a projection of your past onto the present. Discernment is the quiet recognition that something is not aligned—before your life has the evidence to defend that recognition socially.

Fear agitates the system. Discernment stabilises it.

The world teaches you to mistrust what you cannot justify. So when you feel an internal signal without proof, you assume the signal must be emotional noise.

Often, it is not.

1. Fear Is Loud and Fast

Fear is acceleration. It does not wait. It does not observe. It does not pause to gather information or test reality. Its first impulse is movement—any movement—because stillness feels intolerable when control feels threatened.

It rushes. It floods. It multiplies scenarios. It demands immediate relief. It turns uncertainty into urgency. Fear does not ask whether action is wise; it insists that action is necessary. The speed itself becomes the proof. The faster you move, the more convinced you feel that something must be done.

Fear has a particular texture in the body: a racing mind that cannot settle; a need to do something now; a compulsion to check, confirm, interpret; a narrowing of attention until only one outcome exists; the feeling that if you do not act, you will lose control. The body tightens around this belief. Breath shortens. Perspective collapses. Everything becomes about preventing an imagined future from arriving.

Fear does not simply alert you. Fear attempts to manage the future. It tries to outrun uncertainty by forcing resolution, even when resolution is premature. It treats ambiguity as danger and patience as risk.

That management can look like over-explaining, over-texting, over-accommodating, and over-performing. It can look like apologising for needs you have not even spoken. It can look like abandoning your own pace, so the relationship does not leave you behind. Fear convinces you that staying aligned requires constant adjustment—and that any pause might cost you connection.

Fear demands resolution because it cannot tolerate ambiguity. It experiences waiting as exposure and silence as a threat. It pushes you to close the gap before you understand what the gap is asking you to notice.

Fear makes you speed up. And when you speed up, you miss the pattern. You miss repetition. You miss the trajectory. You miss the quiet information that only reveals itself when you slow down enough to watch what happens next.

Fear feels active, but it is reactive. It feels protective, but it often gives away your agency. And this is why learning to recognise its velocity matters—not to shame it, but to stop letting speed decide what deserves your trust.

Because what rushes you rarely has your future in mind.

2. Discernment Is Calm and Steady

Discernment is not acceleration. It is a settling. It does not surge through the body with urgency or demand immediate action. It arrives as a deceleration of noise, a reduction of internal pressure, a quiet reorganisation of attention. Where fear mobilises, discernment stabilises.

Discernment often arrives as a quiet internal boundary—not announced, not dramatic, not explained. There is no speech attached to it, no performance, no need to convince yourself or anyone else. It simply takes shape as an internal line you do not cross, long before you feel compelled to justify why.

It has a different texture: stillness rather than urgency; clarity without adrenaline; a steady no that does not argue; a sense of being less persuadable; an instinct to slow down, not to chase; the feeling that something requires distance, not debate. This texture is unmistakable once you learn it. It does not agitate the nervous system—it steadies it. It does not narrow your vision—it sharpens it.

Discernment does not spin possibilities. It tracks the trajectory. It is not interested in what could be said to repair the moment or smooth the interaction. It watches what has already been happening and projects forward. It notices repetition. It notices the cost. It notices where effort is consistently required from you and where it is not returned.

It does not shout. It weighs. It measures what is sustainable against what is familiar. It considers not just impact, but accumulation. Not just intention, but outcome over time.

Discernment does not need you to act immediately. It simply stops you from moving forward unthinkingly. It reduces your exposure until more information arrives—because it is not trying to win the moment. It is trying to protect your future. It understands that premature action often serves anxiety rather than wisdom.

Fear says: *What if?*
Discernment says: *Notice that.*

Fear pulls you into reaction. Discernment keeps you in observation. Fear demands resolution. Discernment tolerates ambiguity without surrendering clarity.

Fear makes you louder. Discernment makes you quieter. Not because you are confused—because you are watching. Watching how things unfold when you do not rush to explain, fix, or pursue. Watching who respects your pause and who becomes unsettled by it. Watching what emerges when you stop filling the space.

This is why discernment feels calm. It is not detached. It is anchored. It does not need certainty to be effective. It only needs enough accuracy to slow you down before harm has to announce itself.

And once you recognise that calm, steady quality, you stop mistaking urgency for truth—and you stop mistaking intensity for clarity.

2.1. Why Discernment Requires Stillness

Discernment does not emerge in noise.

It requires stillness—not silence as withdrawal, but enough internal quiet to register what is happening without being swept into it. Discernment needs space to track tone, sequence, contradiction, and emotional residue. It needs room to notice not just what is being said, but what is happening to you while it is being said.

This is why discernment often arrives when things slow down. And this is also why certain dynamics work very hard to prevent stillness from ever settling.

When a person does not want your discernment to activate, they do not usually argue against it. They overwhelm it. They keep your system busy—stimulated, flooded, occupied, engaged—so there is no quiet moment for perception to organise itself.

Excessive attention can do this. So can intensity. So can money, sex, constant communication, relentless closeness, or grand declarations that leave no breathing room between moments.

None of these things is harmful in itself. But when they arrive too quickly, too continuously, or too insistently, they serve a different function: they dull your capacity to pause. They keep your nervous system activated just enough that you cannot rest into yourself long enough to notice what is off.

Discernment does not shout over stimulation. It waits for quiet.

Love-bombing, in particular, often works this way. It creates a sense of momentum that prevents you from returning to yourself. You are constantly responding—texts, plans, reassurance, affection—without time to process how you actually feel when the interaction ends. The attention feels flattering, even intoxicating, but it leaves no space to ask a simple question: *How do I feel when I am alone again?*

Without solitude, that question never gets answered.

But stillness is not only environmental. It is internal.

A person who knows themselves—who is familiar with their own inner landscape, their pace, their values, their emotional baseline—does not lose discernment easily, even in intensity. When solitude has been lived, not feared, the self becomes recognisable. And once you recognise yourself, it becomes much harder for someone else to overwrite you.

This is why being at peace with oneself matters. Solitude is not just where you rest—it is where you meet yourself. Where you learn what your thoughts feel like when they are yours. Where you recognise which emotions arise organically and which arrive through pressure. Where you understand your own rhythms well enough to notice when something external is trying to rush, steer, or destabilise them.

Knowing yourself is not self-absorption. It is orientation.

Without knowing yourself, you cannot truly understand others—because you cannot tell what is coming from you and what is being introduced into you. But when self-knowledge is present, even flooding loses its power. You may still feel the intensity, but you can track it. You can say, quietly and internally: *This is not mine.* You can ask, "*What is being activated here?" What is being sought? What is being rushed?*

This is why people who are uncomfortable with their own company are especially vulnerable to intensity. When stillness feels unfamiliar or unsafe, constant stimulation can be mistaken for connection. Movement can be mistaken for meaning. Attention can be mistaken for care.

But discernment lives in the pause.

It appears when there is enough quiet to notice the aftertaste of interaction. Enough space to replay conversations without rationalising them. Enough distance to observe how your body responds when the influence is no longer present.

Anything that denies you that space does not strengthen intuition—it interferes with it.

Discernment does not require deprivation. It requires room.

And when room is repeatedly denied, the nervous system does the only thing it can: it withdraws. Not dramatically. Not angrily. Quietly. Because withdrawal restores the stillness, discernment needs to speak.

2.2. Why Discernment Collapses When Identity Is Unanchored

Because what stillness reveals can be psychologically unaffordable when belonging is your anchor.

Discernment does not fail because people lack intuition. It fails because intuition threatens attachment when identity is externally anchored. This is not a deficit of perception; it is a conflict of survival strategies. The system is not asking, *Is this true?* It is asking, *Can I afford to know this and still belong?*

An anchored self can see clearly. An unanchored one cannot—not because it is unintelligent, but because clarity becomes too expensive. The cost is not information. The cost is loss.

When identity is anchored in another human being, perception is no longer neutral. It becomes negotiable. Reality becomes conditional. Truth becomes something that must be weighed against the risk of loss. What you see is filtered through what you fear losing. What you feel is edited to preserve continuity. What you know is delayed until it feels survivable.

Humans are not stable anchors. They shift. They change. They age. They fracture under pressure. Relationships reorganise. Power moves. Mood fluctuates. Desire fades. Certainty dissolves. When a person's sense of self is secured inside something inherently unstable, judgment cannot remain intact. It bends to preserve attachment. It adapts not toward accuracy, but toward endurance.

This is how discernment is overridden—not violently, not consciously, but structurally. No single choice needs to be made. The system adjusts automatically, quietly, repeatedly, until clarity is no longer accessible without threat.

The body registers trajectory early. It notices pressure, incongruence, asymmetry, and cost. But when identity is externally anchored, those signals are not received as information. They are received as a threat. Not a threat to safety—but a threat to belonging. And belonging, when it carries identity, will be protected at all costs. The system learns that truth is dangerous when it endangers attachment.

This is why people work against their own bodies. Not because they are weak—but because losing the relationship would feel like losing themselves. The body speaks, but the psyche overrides. The signal arrives, but interpretation reframes it as fear, anxiety, overreaction, history, or imagination.

When identity is anchored in a partner, the relationship becomes central rather than contextual. It becomes the reference point through which all meaning is filtered. What threatens the relationship threatens the self. What destabilises the bond destabilises identity. And so perception is edited. Sensation is reinterpreted. Unease is renamed anxiety. Discernment is reframed as fear. The body's signals are treated as a malfunction rather than intelligence. Accuracy becomes suspect; attachment becomes law.

This is not denial. It is preservation. It is the nervous system choosing continuity over coherence.

An unanchored identity cannot afford to see clearly, because clarity would require separation—psychological, emotional, or literal. And separation, when identity has nowhere else to stand, feels like annihilation. It does not feel like a loss of a relationship. It feels like a loss of self.

Silence can surface information, but it cannot hold it.
Without anchoring, clarity appears and disappears, flickers and retreats, surfaces and is overridden.

A person may accurately perceive the signal and still override it because the cost of honouring it feels too high. The nervous system calculates not only danger, but loss. And when loss threatens identity rather than preference, the system chooses attachment over truth. Survival wins over accuracy.

This is why solitude is so dangerous to control-based dynamics. Not because solitude is isolation—but because it reanchors identity internally. It removes the external reference point that required distortion.

In solitude, the self becomes the reference point again. You learn your pace without negotiation. Your thoughts without interruption. Your emotions without inducement. Your baseline without influence. You discover what you feel when nothing is being asked of you. And that familiarity becomes an anchor. Not dramatic. Not performative. Stable.

Once identity is internally anchored, discernment no longer threatens survival. It becomes usable. The body can speak without being overridden. Sensation can register without being argued away. Perception can land without being bargained with. Clarity no longer implies catastrophe.

An anchored person may still feel attachment. They may still love deeply. They may still grieve loss. But they do not lose orientation when pressure arrives. They do not need to distort reality to remain connected. They do not need to negotiate their own perception to preserve belonging. They can hold attachment *and* truth without collapsing.

This is why clarity often arrives alongside grief. Not because something precious is being destroyed—but because something false can no longer be sustained. The grief is not for what was real. It is for what required blindness to survive.

An internally anchored self does not need certainty from others. It does not require validation to trust what it registers. It does not collapse when approval is withdrawn. And because it can survive separation, it can finally see clearly.

This is the quiet difference between intuition that flickers and discernment that holds. One appears briefly and retreats under pressure. The other remains steady because it has ground.

Discernment does not require bravado. It requires somewhere to stand.

And when identity is anchored within, the body's intelligence is no longer a liability—it becomes guidance.

2.3. Why Some People Can Watch Without Sinking

There is a difference between discernment and endurance that many people miss because the surface can look the same. Both can look calm. Both can look patient. Both can look like someone "not reacting".

Discernment stays present without being hooked. Endurance stays present because leaving feels impossible. One remains by choice. The other remains by constraint. One is steady because it has ground. The other is still because it is bracing.

Anchored discernment does not require distance to stay sane. It can remain kind without becoming governable. It can give the benefit of the doubt without handing itself over. It can watch manipulation unfold without needing to prove it in real time, because it does not need the relationship to confirm the self. It does not need agreement to trust what it sees. It does not need immediate confrontation to feel real. It is not performing tolerance. It is tracking truth. It stays oriented inward even while remaining outwardly present.

Dangerous endurance is something else. It looks like patience, but it is actually bargaining. It keeps staying, not because it is clear, but because it is not anchored enough to lose what it is clinging to. It keeps collecting evidence, not to understand, but to justify leaving—because leaving without justification feels like failure. It calls itself discernment, but it is often attachment trying to survive by waiting for permission to be done. The calm is not grounded; it is frozen.

This is why some people can be surrounded by intensity—sex, money, attention, grand language, constant contact—and still remain internally intact. Their discernment does not collapse under flooding because their identity does not live inside the flood. They can stay gentle while still seeing clearly, because their gentleness is not dependence. It is a choice. It is resourced. It is reversible.

They can hold two things at once: *I will not judge you by one moment*, and *I am recording your pattern.* They can keep their tone soft while their perception stays sharp. They can allow time to reveal what they suspect without surrendering their centre—because they have somewhere else to stand. They are not waiting to be convinced of their worth.

And this is the part that matters: that "somewhere else" is the anchor.

An anchor is not a mood. It is not confidence. It is not detachment. It is a location for identity that another human being cannot negotiate. It is what you return to when someone else tries to destabilise your perception. It is what remains intact when someone withdraws approval, escalates pressure, reframes your boundaries, or tries to make your limits feel immoral.

For some people, that anchor is God—because God is not a variable. God does not fluctuate with mood. God does not bargain for access. God does not punish truth. When your identity is secured in something stable, you do not have to cling to unstable people to feel held. You can love without needing to be chosen. You can be present without being possessed. You can release what is unsafe without experiencing it as the collapse of the self.

For others, that anchor may be deeply held principles, an internal moral compass, a strong relationship with solitude, a sense of calling, community, purpose—anything that roots the self beyond the approval of one person. The language differs. The structure does not. The function is the same: your identity is not up for negotiation.

This is why manipulators misread anchored people. They mistake calm for compliance. They mistake kindness for capturability. They mistake silence for ignorance. And because the anchored person does not erupt, does not perform panic, does not rush to accuse, the manipulator often escalates—tightening the grip, increasing the pressure, sharpening the test—believing the strategy is working.

But the anchored person is not being worked on. They are watching.

They are gathering clarity, not permission. They are allowing the pattern to complete itself. And when the pattern becomes undeniable—not emotionally, but structurally—they do not argue. They do not explain. They disengage. The exit is clean because the self is intact. Nothing has to be salvaged.

This is the warning, and it must be said plainly: do not romanticise this stance if you are not anchored. Remaining present around manipulation is not automatically maturity. It is not automatically discernment. If your nervous system is staying because you fear losing them, if your identity is collapsing around their approval, if you cannot sleep, cannot think, cannot feel steady, cannot imagine leaving without bargaining—what you are calling discernment may be dangerous endurance.

Endurance without anchoring is how people disappear inside relationships. It is how harm becomes normal. It is how the body's signals are repeatedly overridden until the signal stops speaking and the person stops recognising themselves. What looks like strength from the outside becomes erosion on the inside.

Anchored discernment does not stay to prove. It stays only as long as it remains free. The moment freedom is threatened, it withdraws—not as punishment, not as retaliation, but as protection.

Because the clearest sign of anchoring is not how long you can tolerate confusion. It is how quickly you can leave once you are no longer confused.

3. Why People Confuse the Two

People confuse fear and discernment because both are signals.

And because many have been trained—especially in love—to treat their own perception as untrustworthy unless it can be justified.

If you were taught that being "good" means being agreeable, you will interpret any internal resistance as selfishness.

If you were taught that love requires endless benefit of the doubt, you will interpret any hesitation as hardness.

If you were taught that conflict is the worst thing, you will label discomfort as anxiety so you can override it.

This confusion is reinforced socially.

A calm woman who pulls back is often treated as unreasonable because she is not performing distress. She is not presenting a dramatic incident. She is not offering a story that people can approve.

She simply withdraws.

And because she cannot produce a headline, people assume her perception is invalid. Discernment rarely arrives with urgency. **That is precisely why it is missed.**

But discernment rarely comes with a headline. **It comes with a pattern.**

This is why you can feel discernment in a relationship that is "nice." A person can be polite and still be positioning. A person can be gentle and still be steering.

Control does not always enter loudly. Sometimes it enters respectfully—through tone, timing, and the slow reorganisation of whose comfort matters most.

Fear reacts to what might happen. Discernment registers what already is.

A Clarifying Distinction

Fear often makes you want closeness to relieve discomfort.
Discernment often makes you want distance to preserve clarity.

Fear tends to increase dependence.
Discernment tends to restore agency.

Fear makes you negotiate your own perception.
Discernment makes you stop negotiating what you feel.

Fear looks like: *pursuit.*
Discernment looks like: *pause.*

Why This Matters

If you mislabel discernment as fear, you will treat your most accurate signals as pathology. You will override yourself in the name of being fair. You will stay in environments that require you to go numb to remain.

If you mislabel fear as discernment, you will punish safe people for the crimes of unsafe ones. You will flee intimacy because it feels vulnerable. You will confuse discomfort with danger.

This happens most often when fear arises not from the present relationship but from an *unintegrated experience*. When harm has not been processed, the nervous system stays alert not for what *is*, but for what it is determined never to experience again. In this state, fear does not seek understanding. *It seeks control.*

Hypervigilance begins to masquerade as wisdom. Suspicion is reframed as insight. Projection is defended as intuition. The person is no longer responding to who is in front of them, but to a memory that has not released its grip. Every neutral action is interpreted. Every ambiguity is filled in. Every difference is treated as a threat—not because danger is present, but because the system is trying to prevent a loss it has already lived through.

This is how safe people become targets. They are not met as they are. They are scanned for resemblance. Their behaviour is read through a template they did not create. They are asked to carry histories, motives, and intentions that belong elsewhere. And because they cannot defend themselves against accusations that are not actually about them, intimacy never forms. What others come to know is not their character, but their survival strategy.

Fear, mislabelled as discernment, often creates the very outcome it claims to be preventing. It erodes trust. It provokes defensiveness. It collapses safety—and then points to the wreckage as proof it was right all along. Meanwhile, the actual sources of harm—those who benefit from confusion, control, or silence—often remain unchallenged. Fear does not expose power. *It displaces it.*

This is why learning the difference matters. **Discernment responds to what is. Fear reacts to what was.** Discernment reduces distortion. Fear multiplies it. Discernment clarifies the relationship. Fear replaces relationship with vigilance.

The goal is not to "trust your intuition" indiscriminately. The goal is to know when you are *seeing clearly*—and when you are trying to feel safe by assigning danger where it does not belong.

Fear is a storm. Discernment is a compass.
Fear demands movement. Discernment demands honesty.

Not honesty with another person first—*honesty with yourself.* Because the earliest form of self-betrayal is not what you do, it is what you dismiss.

And the earliest form of freedom is not drama. It is recognising when your spirit has already stopped consenting—even while your mouth is still trying to be polite.

That is not fear.
That is the beginning of sight.

✦ Calm Unease vs. Panic ✦

Why panic often comes after harm · Why calm resistance appears before it · How safety leaves before danger arrives

Panic is often mistaken for the first warning.

It is not.

Panic is usually what arrives after you have been carrying too much for too long—after your body has spent months negotiating with your mind, after your spirit has been asking you to pause, after your boundaries have been stretched into "patience", after the environment has taught you that truth has consequences. **Panic is a stress response, not a warning system.**

Panic is rarely the beginning.

Panic is the body's emergency response to something it cannot stop politely.

Calm unease is different.
Calm unease is what comes when you are still early enough to choose.

1. Why panic often comes after harm

Panic has a story people recognise. It looks like fear. It sounds like urgency. It has a visible language.

But the body does not panic because it has experienced a single strange moment. **The body goes into panic when it has lost confidence that safety will return.**

Panic tends to appear when:
your reality has been repeatedly minimised;
your *no* has become a negotiation;
your questions have been answered with pressure instead of clarity;
you have been required to stay agreeable in environments that are not reciprocal;
your nervous system has been holding steady while the relationship quietly reorganises itself around someone else.

Panic is not always "overreaction". **Often, it is late recognition.** Because most harm does not arrive in the form of violence, it arrives like an adjustment.

It is what happens when the mind finally stops defending what the body has been enduring.

People often ask, *"Why am I panicking now?"* Because you are no longer in the early stage where distance was available.

Panic is the cost of staying past the first signal.

2. *Why calm resistance appears before it*

Calm resistance is rarely dramatic.

It does not come with rage. It does not come with speeches. It does not come with revenge.

It often comes as an internal shift: you are still kind, but you are no longer pliable. You are still present, but you are no longer easily moved. You still listen, but you stop yielding your reality to maintain peace.

Calm resistance shows up as: taking longer to respond; feeling less persuaded by charm; becoming careful with what you disclose; noticing yourself rehearse sentences before speaking; feeling a quiet not yet when the other person tries to speed the pace; losing the appetite for explaining what should be obvious; no longer offering emotional access on demand; feeling uninterested in proving your goodness; becoming less responsive to urgency; noticing that reassurance no longer reassures; sensing that agreement would cost something you are no longer willing to spend; feeling your body lean back internally even while you remain outwardly polite; recognising that your presence is being managed rather than met; realising that continued openness would require self-distortion.

This is not a withdrawal born of fear. It is resistance born of recognition.

It is the moment your system stops being negotiable. The moment your body quietly revokes consent to dynamics that depend on your flexibility, your doubt, or your over-functioning. It is the body protecting your future while your mind is still searching for words.

It is not fear.

Fear rushes. **Calm resistance slows.**

Fear makes you chase reassurance. **Calm resistance withdraws consent until clarity returns.**

Calm resistance occurs when your system detects that continuing as usual will cost you.

And because it is calm, it is often misunderstood—especially by those who benefit from you being accessible.

To a mutual partner, calm resistance invites care. **To a controlling partner, calm resistance feels like disobedience.**

3. How safety leaves before danger arrives

This is one of the most brutal truths to explain:
Most unsafe dynamics do not begin with danger. **They begin with the departure of safety.**

Safety does not leave with a bang. It leaves by increments.

It leaves when you start managing tone more than truth. It leaves when honesty becomes expensive. It leaves when you feel a mild dread before certain conversations. It leaves when your needs are treated as problems to fix rather than realities to honour. It leaves when your boundaries are reclassified as "attitude". It leaves when your questions are framed as a sign of disrespect.

Nothing "bad" has happened yet.

But something essential has already changed: **your body no longer trusts the environment to hold you.**

The body is not measuring appearances. **It is measuring permission.**

And here is the quiet sign that safety has left: you stop feeling free. Not free to be reckless—*free to be real.* Free to ask without penalty; free to name discomfort without being punished; free to have needs without being accused; free to change your mind without being destabilised; free to take up space without being corrected; free to speak plainly without managing fallout; free to rest without being resented; free to be affected without being framed as weak; free to disagree without being reinterpreted as hostile; free to say no without owing a performance; free to exist without becoming smaller, quieter, simpler—*easier to hold.*

When safety leaves, you do not necessarily feel afraid. **You feel edited**. You begin to pre-empt reactions. You adjust your tone before you know your words. You scan for consequences before you scan for truth. You notice that honesty now requires preparation, that neutrality is read as defiance, that clarity invites consequence.

You realise that access to your full self is no longer welcome—only the parts that cooperate, only the parts that soothe, only the parts that do not disrupt the arrangement.

And this is how safety disappears: *not with a threat, but with a condition.* Not with cruelty, but with cost. Not with force, but with the slow recognition that being fully human here will require self-erasure.

When you are no longer free to be real, you are no longer safe—no matter how calm the surface looks.

When safety leaves, the relationship may still look fine to outsiders. Words may remain polite. Plans may continue. Affection may still appear.

But inside you, the atmosphere shifts.

You begin to monitor. You begin to ration honesty. You begin to conserve your softness—not because you are damaged, but because you are adapting. And *adaptation is not the same thing as intimacy.*

What often confuses people is not what they felt, but the order in which they felt it.

The sequence most people miss

Many people believe the order is:
danger → panic → withdrawal.

But in many relational systems, the order is:
loss of safety → calm unease → quiet resistance → panic (if you override yourself) → exit.

This is why so many people say later, *"I don't know when I stopped feeling close. I just did."* Because safety left early, and your body noticed before your mind could defend it.

A closing truth

Calm unease is not a failure of love. **It is often the first sign that love is being asked to function without protection.**

Panic is not a personality flaw. **It is often the nervous system's final refusal to keep absorbing what your mouth keeps calling "fine".**

If you learn to honour calm unease, you often never need panic to force your hand.

You begin earlier.

Where freedom actually begins.

✦ Where Discernment Lives ✦

The nervous system as witness • Why the body notices incongruence • Why the mind demands justification

Discernment does not live first in your opinions. **It lives in your nervous system.**

Before you have language, you have a bodily register. Before you have proof, you have a felt sense. Before you have a story you can defend, you have a quiet internal shift that says: *something here is not safe to receive naively.*

This is not superstition. **It is witness.**

The nervous system is the first part of you that encounters reality without performing. It does not negotiate for politeness. It does not care how something looks on paper. It does not grant access because a person is charming, credible, admired, spiritual, or "good on paper". It measures what is happening, not what is claimed.

And it measures it relentlessly.

1. The nervous system as witness

Your nervous system is constantly tracking three questions beneath the conversation: *Am I safe here? Am I free here? Is my reality permitted here?*

This is why a relationship can appear calm while your body refuses to settle.

Your nervous system reads the room the way skin reads temperature. It notices whether warmth is genuine or performative. It notices whether attention is care or surveillance. It notices whether closeness is connection—or access.

The witness is not dramatic. **It is consistent.**

You feel it when you are listened to, but not held; included, but not considered; praised, but not protected; wanted, but not honoured; pursued, but not respected.

When your presence is welcomed, but your impact is inconvenient.
When your insight is admired, but your boundaries are resisted.
When your strength is celebrated, but your vulnerability is exploited.
When your labour is relied upon, but your limits are negotiated away.
When your compliance is rewarded, but your autonomy is quietly corrected.
When you are consulted, but decisions are already made.
When you are visible but never authoritative over your own experience.
When you are valued for what you provide, not for what you require.
When your pain is acknowledged in theory, but not altered for in practice. When you are close enough to serve the system, but never

close enough to shape it.

Nothing overt is denied. Nothing explicit is taken. And yet something essential never arrives.

This is how people end up confused rather than alarmed—because the harm is not in what is done, but in *what is systematically withheld.*

This is how the nervous system testifies: **by changing your posture towards the person.**

You start leaning back.

Not as a strategy. **As a verdict.**
Because something in you has already decided it will not go any further.

2. Why the body notices incongruence

The body notices incongruence because incongruence is a power signal.

When words and behaviour align, the system relaxes. You may still disagree, but you feel met. There is coherence. There is safety in consistency.

But when words and behaviour diverge, the body tightens—because contradiction is where manipulation hides.

A person can praise you loudly while quietly hollowing you out. A person can celebrate you in public and diminish you in private. A person can tell you that you are *gifted, special, chosen*—while steadily training you to doubt your own capacity to move without them. A person can say, **"I**

respect you," while treating your questions as inconveniences.

They can admire your potential while obstructing the conditions required for it to grow. They can say, **"I believe in you,"** while arranging conditions in which you cannot advance—*delaying, redirecting, or withholding* every concrete step that would allow that belief to materialise. They can say, **"I support your gifts,"** while discouraging the very environments where those gifts would be affirmed, sharpened, or seen. They can frame themselves as your greatest supporter while positioning themselves as the *sole gateway* to resources, opportunity, permission, or progress.

A person can make you feel exceptional—and then make sure you feel incapable without them.

They may praise your independence while punishing your autonomy. They may applaud your ambition while ensuring the timing is never right, the funds are never available, and the approval is never quite given. They may insist all money must flow through them **"for order," "for wisdom," "for protection,"** while ensuring that every meaningful step forward requires *their permission, their timing, or their account.* Not by refusal—but by delay. Not by saying no—but by making yes impossible. They can say, **"I'm protecting you,"** while quietly isolating you from opportunity. They can say, **"This is for your own good,"** while steadily eroding your confidence, momentum, and trust in yourself. They can say, **"We're building together,"** while designing a future in which only one person has mobility, safety, or expansion.

What makes this effective—and dangerous—is that it is *deniable.* The praise is genuine. The gestures can be listed. The words can be repeated. The record can be defended. The story of support can be told convincingly. And yet the outcome remains unchanged: *you do not advance.* You become smaller, slower, less certain, and more dependent. Your confidence erodes. Your momentum dies. Your world narrows. You begin to feel that survival depends on *their mood, permission, account, and timing*. Your life does not open. **It contracts.**

This is how dependency is built: *not by breaking you outright, but by convincing you that you cannot stand without the person who is quietly kneecapping you.*

The body recognises this long before the mind does, not as a thought, but as tension. It tightens not because it is confused, but because it is registering a pattern: elevation paired with obstruction; affection paired with restriction; praise paired with paralysis.

Contradiction is not incidental here. Contradiction is the mechanism.

Incongruence is not always lying in the obvious sense. Often it is subtler: a mismatch between *tone and intention*, between *affection and accountability*, between *promises and structure*, between *closeness and care.*

The mind hears the vow. **The body feels the direction.**

The body notices when affection is used to soften you while terms are being introduced to bind you. It notices when warmth is deployed before a difficult demand. It notices when conflict appears not as a shared problem, but as an inconvenience to be managed—because *management replaces mutuality when control is present.*

This is why some relationships leave you tired without visible drama.

Your body has been doing *unpaid labour*: translating, adapting, bracing, preparing, trying to stay safe inside contradictions.

And the cost of living inside contradiction is always paid in the body first.

3. Why the mind demands justification

The mind is trained for social survival. The body is trained for physiological survival. These are not always aligned. The mind learns how to remain acceptable; the body learns how to remain intact. One prioritises belonging, coherence, and reputation. The other prioritises safety, continuity, and regulation. When these priorities diverge, tension begins inside the self.

Your mind wants a case, because a case earns permission. A case makes you believable. A case protects you from being called irrational. The mind does not simply want truth—it wants truth that can survive scrutiny, debate, and dismissal. It wants a version of reality that can be defended in public, even if that defence costs you private peace.

Most people were trained—especially in love—to be fairer than they are safe. To wait for proof. To gather evidence. To explain themselves properly. To avoid "overreacting". To give grace. This training is often praised as maturity, generosity, and emotional intelligence. But beneath it sits a quieter lesson: your discomfort is not enough on its own. Your instinct does not count unless it can be justified.

The mind demands justification because it is afraid of being wrong in public. It fears the social consequences of choosing yourself without consensus. It fears being seen as unreasonable, dramatic, difficult, or unstable. It is afraid of standing alone with an experience that cannot yet be proven.

It asks: What if I misread it? What if I'm being unfair? What if it's just my past? What if I ruin something good? What if I can't explain it and people judge me? Each question sounds like caution, but together they form a pattern of self-interruption. The mind interrogates perception not to refine it, but to delay action until permission arrives.

So the mind does what it knows how to do: it builds arguments against your own perception. It edits sensation into palatability. It reframes a warning into doubt. It translates embodied knowledge into hypotheses that can be postponed. It keeps you engaged long after your system has already begun to withdraw.

It looks for reasons to stay open when your body is closing. It looks for explanations when your system is trying to set the distance. It looks for certainty when discernment is asking for restraint. The mind seeks clarity that can be defended; the body seeks distance that can be felt.

This is why many people do not exit when the body first signals. They exit when the mind finally receives enough evidence to justify what the body already knew. The leaving is not sudden—it is overdue. The decision is not impulsive—it is delayed.

By then, the body has been carrying the discrepancy alone. Holding tension. Holding vigilance. Holding the cost of staying present while not feeling safe. The body does not argue its case. It endures. And when the mind finally agrees, it is often not relief that arrives first—but exhaustion.

Because the truth did not need justification, it required trust.

The gap that costs people years

There is a quiet interval during which most damage occurs. Not at the beginning, when things still feel open. Not at the end, when leaving becomes unavoidable. But in the space between knowing and acting—between what the body registers immediately and what the mind insists must be justified. This gap is rarely acknowledged, yet it is where people lose time, vitality, and self-trust.

This is the gap: the body says, **"Something is off."** The mind says, **"Prove it."**

That demand for proof sounds reasonable. It wears the language of fairness, maturity, and restraint. But it creates a delay that benefits only one thing: the continuation of the arrangement as it is. While proof is gathered, the system remains intact. While evidence is assembled, the cost continues to accrue.

In healthy environments, you do not need to prove your discomfort to remain worthy of care. Your questions are welcome. Your pace is respected. Your boundaries do not trigger punishment. Discomfort is treated as information, not as an accusation. It is met with curiosity rather than correction.

In control-based environments, you are required to justify your instincts because your instincts threaten the arrangement. They interrupt efficiency. They destabilise hierarchy. They reintroduce agency where compliance was expected. So the burden is shifted onto you—not to feel less, but to explain more.

And this is why the most dangerous dynamics are not always the loud ones. They do not announce themselves with volatility or overt harm. They arrive quietly, wrapped in civility.

They are the ones where you are made to feel unreasonable for noticing. Where the terms are introduced slowly. Where the language is polite, the tone is calm, and the cost keeps rising. Where nothing is explicitly wrong, yet everything becomes heavier, where your intuition is treated as a problem to be solved rather than a signal to be honoured.

The mind keeps waiting for a moment significant enough to deserve leaving. The body keeps recording the cost of staying.

One is looking for justification. The other is keeping the ledger.

What discernment looks like before it has words

Before discernment becomes a decision, it becomes a posture. Long before there is clarity, there is orientation. The body begins to reposition itself in subtle, non-dramatic ways—often misunderstood as withdrawal, moodiness, or distance.

You stop over-sharing. You stop explaining what should be obvious. You begin watching timing and tone. You conserve your softness. You notice relief in distance. You feel your yes become harder to access. None of this is reactive. None of it is strategic. It is not punishment. It is preservation.

This is not avoidance. This is the nervous system testifying. It is responding to information the mind has not yet authorised.

It is saying: **I have begun to detect a pattern that will require self-erasure to sustain.**

That sentence does not arrive as language at first. It arrives as sensation. As fatigue after contact. As tension before engagement. As a quiet preference for space that feels like relief rather than loss.

And no healthy love requires you to disappear to stay connected.

Discernment does not begin with confrontation. It starts with the refusal to keep betraying what you already feel. And once that refusal starts—however quietly—the trajectory has already changed.

A closing truth

Discernment is not paranoia. **It is coherence.**

It is the part of you that notices when the relationship is becoming less mutual and more managed—before you have the social evidence to defend your knowing.

The nervous system is not trying to make you suspicious. **It is trying to keep you whole.**

And when it begins to withdraw, it is not always because something terrible has happened.

Sometimes it is because something is forming.

And you are allowed to trust what forms inside you—even before you can justify it to anyone else.

Because the earliest sign of an unsafe environment is not the presence of danger.

It is the absence of permission.

Permission to be real. Permission to have needs. Permission to say no without consequence. Permission to exist without becoming smaller.

Discernment lives where that permission is measured.

And the body measures first.

By now, you have not been asked to judge anyone. You have not been asked to decide what something "is". You have only been asked to notice what your body noticed first: discomfort, unease, withdrawal, the quiet sense that something was reorganising itself around you.

Part I stayed close to sensation because that is where truth appears earliest. But sensation alone is not enough. What the body detects is not random. It is responding to something specific—something structured.

The body does not react without cause. **It reacts to systems.**

And what the body sensed was not simply a mood, or a misunderstanding, or poor communication.

It was an early shift in power.

To understand why your instincts were so precise, you must now look at what they were responding to.

II

✦ HOW CONTROL ACTUALLY WORKS ✦

Mechanisms, not personalities

Part II moves from perception to structure.
It is not about personalities or pathology, but about architecture.
Control rarely begins with force; it begins with access.
It arrives as care, patience, or inevitability.

These chapters examine how imbalance is quietly built—through attachment,
silence, negotiation, and structure—long before harm is visible,
and why the body sensed it first.

✦ Tether Before Domination ✦

Why attachment comes before demands · Why charm precedes entitlement · Why access is established early

Control rarely begins with control. **It begins with tether.**

Not a chain you can see, but a bond you can feel: familiarity, emotional rhythm, routine contact, the steady feeling of being chosen. Something in you starts to organise itself around their presence. You begin to anticipate them. You begin to make room.

That is the first stage: not domination—**positioning**.

Because domination is expensive at the beginning, it risks rejection. It exposes intent too early. So the strategy, where it exists, is seldom to demand first. The strategy is to attach first—to create a relationship you will hesitate to disrupt.

A tether does not need to be dramatic. **It needs to be repeated.**

A tether is established through small, consistent access: **frequent contact that becomes normal; emotional closeness that feels protective; shared language that creates an inside world; personal disclosures**

that invite yours; responsiveness that trains trust; attention that feels like safety; help that arrives during vulnerability; support that stabilises uncertainty; guidance that slowly replaces choice; care that positions itself as authority; provision that begins to expect compliance; rescue that quietly rewrites the terms of belonging.

At first, the access feels benevolent. You are grateful. Relieved. Held. Someone has stepped in where life felt unstable. Decisions feel lighter because someone else is carrying them. Direction feels clearer because it is being offered with confidence. What is rarely named is that this help does not merely support your life — **it begins to redirect it**. Sometimes the redirection does not come through help at all. It comes through definition.

You begin to be named before you are constrained. *The reasonable one. The strong one. The calm one. The one who understands. The one who doesn't make things difficult.* An identity is quietly assigned—and then protected.

Once this happens, your range narrows without instruction. Certain emotions no longer fit who you are "supposed" to be. Certain questions feel out of character. Certain needs begin to feel like violations of the role you've been given.

This is not overt control. It is subtler. You are not told what you cannot do. You simply learn who you are expected to remain. And once your belonging is tied to that identity, deviation feels dangerous. Not because someone stops you—but because becoming yourself fully now threatens the bond itself.

Paths you were already walking are paused "for now". **Delay be-**

comes the governing language. Not refusal—postponement. Not opposition—caution. Not prohibition—timing.

The future is always acknowledged and endlessly deferred. *Not yet. Let's wait. After this settles. Once things are more stable. When the moment is right.* Progress is never denied—only delayed until momentum quietly dissolves.

Over time, the initiative begins to feel premature. Desire begins to feel irresponsible. Movement begins to feel like pressure. You start asking permission for steps you once took naturally.

This is how autonomy is slowed without force. Nothing is forbidden. Everything is simply not the right time. And because no clear no is ever spoken, it becomes difficult to name what is being lost—until years have passed and nothing has moved.

Capacities you were already developing are deferred "until later". **Your future is reorganised under the logic of care.**

Over time, the help gains gravity. Movement begins to require permission. Independence is reframed as risk. Initiative becomes "too much, too soon". Questions are met with reminders of what was done for you. The past is quietly edited: *what you were building before is minimised; your agency before intervention is erased; your survival is retold as rescue.* Gratitude becomes an expectation. Dependence becomes proof of loyalty.

Another tether forms through emotional climate.

You begin to sense which truths create distance, which questions cool the room, which needs introduce tension. You learn when silence preserves harmony and when honesty costs connection. Without being told, you start managing the atmosphere.

You soften language—you time disclosures. You postpone conversations. You carry discomfort alone to keep things calm.

This is not mutual attunement. **It is emotional labour performed in one direction.**

The relationship remains "peaceful," but only because one person is regulating it. And the more skilled you become at maintaining that peace, the less room there is for your unedited self.

Here, safety is not enforced through punishment—but through withdrawal, not through threats—but through mood. And the tether tightens because staying connected now requires constant self-adjustment.

Resistance is no longer read as self-protection, but as ingratitude. The moment you push back, the story shifts—not to what is being controlled, but to who you supposedly were without them. Your history is recast to justify your containment. Your hesitation becomes betrayal. Your boundaries become evidence of character failure. And the more your life contracts, the more the narrative insists you would have nothing without the structure that is now restricting you.

Once closeness has a rhythm, interruption becomes leverage.

Not because the care was fake, but because it was conditional. Not because the support was imagined — but because it came with authorship claims. The tether tightens not through cruelty, but through *redefinition*: of who you were, what you're allowed to want, and how much autonomy you're permitted to retain.

And once the tether is formed, subsequent demands no longer feel like demands. **They feel like the price of staying connected.**

This is why many people cannot name the moment things changed. The tether was built in a season that looked like intimacy.

That is the groundwork. Now we can name the mechanics.

Why attachment comes before demands

Demand without attachment gets refused. **Demand with attachment gets negotiated.**

Once a bond exists, the person being pressured is no longer making decisions from neutral ground. They are making decisions based on investment: time, emotional meaning, and hope. They are making decisions with loss in the room.

This is what tethering accomplishes: **it introduces cost**.

Not always financial cost. Often psychological cost: *If I say no, will I lose the relationship? If I challenge this, will I be punished? If I insist on fairness, will I be accused of being difficult? If I take up space, will they withdraw?*

These questions do not appear in healthy intimacy. **They occur when attachment is being used as leverage.**

Attachment itself is not the problem. Attachment is human. **The**

problem arises when attachment is engineered to allow an imbalance to be installed later without immediate revolt.

A tether makes you easier to move—not because you are weak, but **because you are connected.**

And once attachment is secured, something subtle happens: you begin regulating yourself before you are asked. You soften questions. You delay refusals. You manage tone. You edit your needs. Not because you were instructed to—but because preserving the bond has become part of your nervous system's job.

That self-regulation is the tether doing its work.

Why charm precedes entitlement

Charm is not always deception. Many charming people are simply warm.

But in control-based dynamics, charm often functions as insulation. **It builds credibility. It creates a benefit of the doubt. It establishes an image that later behaviour will hide behind.** Once that image is formed, discomfort becomes less believable—even to you.

Charm does not just win you. **It wins the environment around you:** friends who say, *"He seems so lovely."* Families who say, *"You're lucky."* Even your own mind is saying, *"Maybe I'm being unfair."*

Charm does more than create intimacy. It creates cover.

Because when a person is widely perceived as kind, generous, spiritual, or selfless, that perception begins to operate as a shield. Harm no longer lands on neutral ground. It lands against a reputation that has already been decided.

Cruelty, when it appears, is often private. Selective. Confined to the person who has the least credibility and the most to lose. The warmth is public. The generosity is visible. The patience is performed for witnesses. What happens behind closed doors is framed as an exception—or denied entirely.

This is why, when someone finally speaks, the response is so often disbelief. Not because the harm is unclear, but because the image is already fixed. The story has been told in advance. And it does not include you as a reliable narrator.

Charm does not just make entitlement easier to introduce. It makes testimony harder to believe.

It ensures that when you describe what happened, people search your tone for instability instead of your words for truth. It trains the room to protect the image rather than examine the structure. And it leaves the person who was targeted isolated not only from safety, but from credibility.

This is how charm becomes a second tether: not to you, but to the world around you. And once that tether is secured, exposure itself becomes a risk—because the system now has more witnesses invested in its innocence than in your reality.

Charm accelerates trust without requiring proof. It invites closeness before the relationship's structure has been tested. It collapses time—

the very thing discernment needs most.

That is why charm often precedes entitlement. Entitlement cannot arrive raw. **It must arrive under protection.**

Once the impression is established, entitlement can wear softer clothes: *"That's just how I am." "You know what I need." "If you loved me, you would..." "As my partner, you should..." "This is what marriage means."*

The words may be calm. **The posture is not.**

A person oriented toward mutuality uses closeness to deepen understanding. A person oriented toward control uses closeness to secure advantage.

Why access is established early

Control is not primarily about love. **It is about access.**

Access to your time, energy, softness, labour, body, resources, and future.

That is why the early phase often contains subtle tests—not of love, but of compliance. Often "reasonable" ones: How quickly will you respond? How much will you explain? How easily will you rearrange? How comfortable are you with saying no? Do you feel guilty for having needs? Will you defend your reality—or apologise for it?

Access is established through normalisation. A thing becomes *"our rhythm"* before you realise it is also their advantage. By the time you notice, it feels rude to change it.

This is how access becomes entitlement: **what you allowed becomes what is expected**.

And expectation becomes a quiet form of coercion. You begin managing their reaction before you even choose your action.

That is the point of tethering: **pre-compliance.**

The moment the tether reveals itself

You rarely discover the tether in the sweet season. **You discover it at the first real interruption.**

The first slowdown. The first refusal. The first boundary that alters the rhythm.

This is where many women are shocked by the disproportionate response.

A simple no produces irritation. A reasonable question produces defensiveness. A request for clarity produces withdrawal. A need for fairness gives rise to moral language, spiritual language, and character attacks.

This is the moment the tether shows its purpose.

Because, in **mutual love**, your "*no*" is **information**. In **control-based dynamics**, your *no* is **defiance**. And **defiance must be corrected**.

Not always with force—often with something quieter, more socially acceptable, and harder to name: *sulking; emotional distance; sudden coolness; clipped responses; strategic silence; dismissal framed as maturity; contempt softened by humour; withdrawal disguised as "needing space"; withholding affection; delaying responses; becoming busy when you need clarity; changing the subject until the issue dies; minimising the concern; reframing your boundary as overreaction; invoking timing ("not now"); invoking tone ("it's how you said it"); invoking loyalty ("after everything I've done"); invoking roles ("that's not how a wife/partner behaves"); invoking reasonableness ("let's not make this bigger than it is"); invoking exhaustion ("I don't have the energy for this"); invoking finality ("I've said my piece"); invoking threat without stating it ("do what you feel is right"); invoking withdrawal as consequence ("we'll talk later"); invoking certainty as authority ("this isn't up for discussion"); invoking moral high ground ("I would never do this to you"); invoking normalisation ("this is how relationships work"); invoking erasure ("you're reading too much into it"); invoking shame ("I didn't realise you were like this"); invoking abandonment cues ("maybe we want different things"); invoking replacement ("someone else wouldn't have a problem with this"); invoking silence until compliance returns.*

The words themselves vary. The lesson does not.

Your reality has consequences here.

Once that lesson is learned, the tether tightens—because you begin editing yourself in advance.

A sober distinction

A mutual attachment makes you freer in love. **An engineered attachment makes you more careful.**

One expands you. **The other manages you.**

This is why tethering comes before domination. Domination works best when you are already bonded, already invested, already carrying the emotional cost of leaving.

Control does not begin by taking your freedom. **It begins by teaching you that using your freedom will cost you something you cannot afford to lose.**

That is tether.

And once you can see it, you stop mistaking early intensity for safety and early closeness for mutuality.

You begin watching for the simplest proof of all:
Does closeness make you freer—or does it make you more careful?

✦ Silence as Rehearsal ✦

When silence is not confusion • How non-response recalibrates strategy • Why bodies feel "watched" instead of met

Silence is often misread as emptiness. As confusion. As avoidance. As someone who does not know what to say. It is interpreted as a lack of thought, of feeling, of capacity. It is treated as an absence, as if nothing is happening, simply because nothing is being spoken.

But in many control-based dynamics, silence is not empty at all. It is **active**. It is deliberate. It is doing work.

Silence is not the absence of response. It is the presence of **assessment**. Silence is not always confusion. Sometimes it is **calibration**—the quiet recalculation of power once something has shifted.

To understand silence, you must distinguish absence from intention.

When silence is not confusion

Confusion looks disorganised. It wavers. It reaches. It circles back with questions. Confusion seeks resolution because it does not yet know what position to take. It is unsettled by not knowing and seeks to restore coherence through dialogue.

Strategic silence behaves differently. It arrives cleanly. It holds. It does not ask. It does not clarify. It does not repair. It simply withdraws engagement while maintaining proximity. It stays close enough to be felt, but distant enough to avoid exposure. It is not lost—it is *watching*.

This kind of silence often appears after something specific: a boundary, a question, a refusal, a moment of fairness. Not a dramatic confrontation—just a shift where you stop yielding automatically. Where something that was once implicit is no longer guaranteed.

The silence that follows is not uncertainty. It is a **calculation**. It is information-gathering. It is the system registering resistance and determining response.

It is the moment where the system pauses to observe how much resistance it is encountering—and how much pressure will be required next. It is a holding pattern, not a collapse.

If silence were confusion, it would feel scattered. Instead, it feels controlled. It has weight. It has a temperature. You are not met with curiosity. You are met with **stillness that carries consequence**.

And that is how you know the silence is not about not knowing what to say.

It is about deciding what to do.

How non-response recalibrates strategy

Silence functions as a test—not of your patience, but of your positioning. It is not waiting; it is measuring. It is not absence; it is appraisal.

It asks questions without asking them out loud: *Will you fill the gap? Will you soften your stance to restore the connection? Will you apologise for creating discomfort? Will you over-explain to earn re-entry? Will you retreat from your boundary to relieve tension?* These questions are not spoken because they do not need to be. The silence itself is the mechanism.

Silence gives the other person space to watch what you do when they withhold engagement. It turns the relational field into an experiment, where your responses supply the data.

Do you stay steady—or do you compensate?

If you compensate, the silence has done its job. It has taught the system exactly how to regain leverage. It has revealed which internal alarms it can activate to produce compliance without confrontation.

This is why silence is often paired with ambiguity rather than departure. The person does not leave. They remain visible, reachable, "around". They stop responding fully. Presence without reciprocity. Access without warmth.

This keeps the tether intact while introducing consequence. The bond remains, but the cost of maintaining it quietly shifts onto you.

The message is not spoken. It is trained: **connection is conditional, engagement must be earned, and resistance has a cost**.

Silence rehearses compliance without demanding it outright.

Why bodies feel "watched" instead of met

One of the most evident signs that silence is strategic rather than confused is how it feels in the body. This is not an intellectual recognition; it is a somatic one.

You do not feel missed. You feel monitored.

There is a difference.

When someone is overwhelmed or unsure, their distance feels neutral or sad. There is an absence, but not pressure. The space feels empty rather than charged.

Strategic silence feels different. You feel suspended, observed and held in a kind of quiet tension. The stillness has gravity.

Your body senses that the other person is not disengaged—they are waiting, waiting to see how much you will adjust yourself to restore equilibrium—waiting to see whether you will self-correct.

This is why people describe feeling "on edge" rather than lonely. Why they replay conversations. Why they consider sending follow-up messages they do not actually believe in. The mind starts working to relieve the pressure the body has already detected.

The nervous system recognises **surveillance**, not absence.

You are still in the field. You are just no longer being met.
And that distinction matters.

Silence as behavioural conditioning

Silence teaches through omission. It does not say, "You were wrong." It lets the discomfort do the teaching. It outsources correction to your nervous system.

The body learns: *asking questions leads to disconnection; naming discomfort leads to withdrawal; fairness disrupts harmony; clarity costs closeness.*

No argument is required. No justification is offered. The silence itself becomes the feedback loop. The learning is implicit, embodied, and therefore difficult to dispute.

This is why silence is such an effective rehearsal tool. It prepares the ground for later escalation by first training the nervous system to associate self-expression with loss. It lowers resistance before any explicit demand is made.

By the time words return, the structure has already shifted.

Why silence often precedes negotiation

Silence is rarely the end. It is the pause before the next move. It is the holding phase between disruption and consolidation.

Once silence has established its effect—once you have demonstrated whether you will self-correct or not—the system adjusts. It does not guess; it calculates.

If you capitulate, silence recedes. If you hold, silence escalates.

This escalation may look like: sudden "let's talk" conversations framed as reasonableness; reframing your boundary as a problem to be solved; invoking fairness, balance, or compromise; introducing terms under the guise of communication.

Silence softens resistance so negotiation can land with force. It reduces your internal certainty, so external structure can appear reasonable.

By the time negotiation appears, your body may already be tired. You may already be second-guessing yourself. You may already want relief from the tension.

That is not accidental.

Silence prepares the terrain.

The critical distinction

Silence that is confusion seeks clarity. Silence that is control seeks an outcome.

One invites conversation—the other conditions behaviour. One creates space. The other creates pressure.

And your body often knows the difference long before your mind does.

If silence makes you feel smaller, more careful, more self-monitoring—if it makes you rehearse apologies instead of truths—it is not neutral.

It is instructive.

A closing truth

Silence is often described as passive. In these dynamics, it is anything but.

Silence is rehearsal.

It is where the system practises removing warmth without removing access. It teaches you the cost of disrupting the arrangement, without yet saying what the arrangement is.

By the time words return, your nervous system has already been trained.

Silence is often described as passive.

Silence prepares the terrain, which is why the next chapter matters.

Because when silence no longer works, the system speaks. And when it speaks, it calls it negotiation. **Not to restore mutuality—but to formalise control.**

✦ Negotiation Is the Final Warning ✦

Why fairness triggers escalation · Why "let's talk about it" provokes attack · Why negotiation precedes exit.

Negotiation is often mistaken for progress. It sounds mature. Reasonable. Safe. It carries the language of partnership: *let's talk, let's align, let's be fair*. It gestures toward collaboration and implies goodwill. But in control-based dynamics, negotiation is not the beginning of repair. It is the **final warning**. It is the moment the system realises that what was once absorbed quietly is about to be examined openly.

Negotiation signals that something has shifted. That compliance is no longer automatic. That silence is no longer available. It announces the arrival of agency. And agency, once expressed, cannot be unseen.

Negotiation is the moment power is forced to explain itself.

Why fairness triggers escalation

Fairness is neutral only in systems that are already equal. In systems organised around advantage, fairness is destabilising. It interferes with the flow of benefit. It disrupts the cost distribution. When you introduce reciprocity—shared risk, shared power, shared protection—you are not asking for improvement. You are challenging the **structure**.

And structure resists exposure.

So the request itself creates a shift that feels disproportionate—the air changes. The tone tightens. The warmth thins. Something closes. You are no longer discussing behaviour, logistics, or feelings. You are touching the **architecture**—the underlying design that determines who adjusts, who absorbs, who pays.

Fairness implies that power should be shared. Control depends on power remaining uneven. So fairness does not land as collaboration. It lands as a **threat**. Not because it is unreasonable, but because it makes visible what the system requires to continue functioning.

Why "Let's Talk About It" Provokes Attack

In healthy relationships, conversation expands understanding. It increases shared reality. It allows both people to orient themselves more accurately to each other. In control-based dynamics, conversation collapses leverage.

Because once something is spoken plainly, it can be examined. Once it is examined, it can be named. And once it is named, it cannot operate invisibly. Ambiguity is not an accident in these systems; it is a resource.

That is why "let's talk about it" often triggers one of three responses, each designed to reassert control rather than address substance:

- **Deflection** — changing the subject, minimising the issue, flooding

you with irrelevancies
- **Reversal** — shifting focus onto your tone, your timing, your character
- **Escalation** — anger, withdrawal, contempt, moral framing

Different tactics. Same objective.

Each response serves the same function. The goal is not resolution. The goal is **containment**. To prevent the conversation from reaching the point at which the structure itself would have to be justified.

Negotiation threatens to restore **mutual reality**. And mutual reality is dangerous to any system that survives on ambiguity. When ambiguity disappears, leverage disappears with it. When leverage disappears, domination cannot be maintained without force.

Negotiation exposes the system.

Negotiation assumes shared intention. But control is not a disagreement about preferences. It is a disagreement over **who has the authority to decide**. One assumes a typical horizon. The other assumes a fixed hierarchy. One believes outcomes are co-created. The other believes outcomes are owned.

When you negotiate in good faith, you reveal something essential: you believe the other person is oriented toward mutuality. You believe they are capable of shared reality, shared power, shared consequence. You are not merely asking for an adjustment; you are signalling *trust*. Their response reveals whether that belief was ever safe.

If they wanted a partnership, negotiation would feel **relieving**. It would lower pressure. It would clarify expectations. It would distribute responsibility. It would feel like alignment.

If they wanted control, negotiation feels **intolerable**. It introduces uncertainty where certainty was assumed. It invites examination where invisibility was required. It implies limits where entitlement had gone unquestioned.

This is why behaviour sharpens after a fair question. Not because the question is provocative, but because it is *diagnostic*. What was once subtle becomes clear. What was once polite becomes cold. What was once flexible becomes rigid. The shift is not emotional; it is structural. The mask drops because it is no longer useful.

Because the system has been observed, it cannot rely on ambiguity to survive. Visibility changes everything. The moment you recognise design instead of intention, pattern instead of exception, the relationship can no longer pretend it is something it is not.

This is the moment many people misinterpret as failure.

Why negotiation precedes exit

Negotiation is often the last attempt to restore balance before the body disengages. This is not indecision and not weakness. It is the final diagnostic act of a system that has been trying—often quietly, often for a long time—to stay relational without self-erasure. Not because the person wants to leave—but because something in them requires confirmation. Something deeper than logic, deeper than hope, deeper than optimism. The nervous system wants proof. The psyche wants coherence. The heart wants to know whether what it has been investing in is capable of meeting it back.

Negotiation asks one final question: **Can this structure hold equality?** Not temporarily. Not rhetorically. Not in intention. But structurally. Can it survive shared power, shared protection, shared consequence—without retaliation, withdrawal, or reassertion of hierarchy once the moment passes?

The answer arrives not in promises, but in posture. Not in words, but in orientation. Not in reassurance, but in response. Bodies answer faster than language ever will. They register whether openness expands or contracts, whether curiosity replaces defensiveness, whether the field widens—or snaps shut.

If negotiation is met with curiosity, repair is possible. Curiosity signals permeability. It signals that power can move, that assumptions can be questioned, that the system can be reshaped without collapsing. Curiosity means the structure can tolerate reality entering the room without punishment.

If it is met with punishment, clarity arrives. Not emotional clarity, but **structural clarity**. The kind that closes a chapter even while the relationship technically continues. The kind that settles something internally so completely that further effort would feel dishonest rather than hopeful.

This is why so many people leave shortly after "the talk". Not because the conversation failed—**because it succeeded**. It revealed what would never change. It delivered the information the body had been waiting for. It resolved ambiguity.

And once ambiguity is resolved, the body no longer negotiates.

The escalation sequence

In many dynamics, the progression looks like this:

Unease is dismissed.
Silence is endured.
Negotiation is attempted.
Escalation appears.

The escalation may be loud or deceptively calm. It may arrive as chaos or as chilling composure. It may look emotional or impressively rational. But its function is the same. It reasserts hierarchy.

It may arrive as:
ultimatums disguised as standards,
moral language used as a weapon,
spiritual framing that makes dissent "rebellion",
sudden coldness where there was once softness,
withdrawal presented as maturity,
and certainty spoken as authority.

Each move communicates the same message: *discussion is over.* The question has been answered. The cost of equality has been calculated—and rejected.

At this stage, the system is no longer testing you. It is **declaring terms**. It is no longer asking who you are. It informs you of what you must accept to remain.

And this is the point at which leaving is no longer a failure of love. It is a **recognition of reality**.

Why negotiation feels dangerous in the body

By the time negotiation happens, the body often already knows the outcome. This is not intuition as mysticism; it is perception as accumulation. Long before a conversation is scheduled, rehearsed, or framed as "necessary," the body has been running its own analysis—quietly, continuously, without commentary.

This is why people describe feeling steady going into the conversation—then strangely clear afterwards. Not relieved, not hopeful, not energised, but resolved. Something settles. Something stops reaching. What appears to be calm is not optimism; it is finality without drama. The body is no longer bracing for a different result.

The nervous system has been tracking patterns long before language caught up. It has been registering tone, timing, responsiveness, and safety. It has noticed what happens when you ask, when you pause, when you need, when you disagree. It has logged how repair is handled, how power moves, how equality is tolerated—or not. None of this required conscious analysis. It only needed exposure.

Negotiation forces the pattern to reveal itself out loud, in real time, where it can no longer hide behind interpretation or hope. When the pattern is spoken into the room, it either adapts—or it defends. There is no third option. Negotiation does not create the outcome; it confirms it.

When the response shows intolerance for equality, the body stops trying.

Not dramatically. Not angrily. Quietly. This quiet is often misread as detachment or emotional shutdown, but it is neither. It is recognition. Effort drains away. The vigilance dissolves. The internal negotiations end. The running commentary—*Maybe if I say it differently, maybe if I wait, maybe if I soften*—falls silent.

The body recognises that further investment will not alter the structure; it will only increase costs. And the body is precise about cost. It measures tension, fatigue, self-monitoring, and the gradual erosion of ease. Once the cost is clear, persistence becomes unnecessary.

This is the moment effort ends. Not because the person gives up, but because the body understands there is nothing left to do.

Not because hope failed—but because accuracy arrived.

The meaning of the final warning

Negotiation is not a failure. It is a **diagnostic**. It is the moment where ambiguity collapses into information.

It tells you whether the relationship is organised around **partnership** or **permission**. Whether power can move, or whether it must be obeyed.

If fairness provokes pressure, the system cannot tolerate equality. If clarity produces punishment, the system requires compliance. If your voice becomes the problem, the structure was never mutual. These are not emotional reactions; they are structural disclosures.

At that point, staying becomes endurance rather than love. It becomes adaptation, not intimacy. And the body knows the difference long before the mind is willing to admit it.

What feels like collapse is often confirmation.
Here is the truth negotiation reveals—cleanly, without theatrics, without cruelty, without drama:

When a person is invested in mutuality, fairness is **relief**.
When a person is invested in dominance, fairness is **humiliation**.

And humiliation does something specific within control-based identities. It converts a simple question into a threat, a boundary into disrespect, and equality into loss. It exposes the dependency on imbalance. It reveals that power was never relational—it was positional.

Which is why negotiation often ends the same way: not with agreement, but with **rage**. Not because the conversation was mishandled, but because the system was confronted.

Because rage is not always an emotion, it may reflect the system's defence.

And once you understand that, you know why fairness provokes it—and why, in the next chapter, we will name what happens when equality enters a structure that requires hierarchy to survive.

✦ Why Fairness Provokes Rage ✦

Equality as a threat · Mutuality as loss of advantage · Why some systems require hierarchy to function

Rage Is Not Always a Feeling

Rage is not always a feeling. Sometimes it is a *function.* Sometimes it is a mechanism. Sometimes it is the reflex that a **control-based system** deploys when a *fair question* enters the room and refuses to leave. Because fairness does not merely request better behaviour, it introduces a principle the system cannot tolerate: **equality**. And equality is not a preference to a hierarchy—it is an **existential threat**.

In a hierarchy, power must remain uneven to remain meaningful. Roles must stay fixed. Advantage must stay protected. When you ask a fair question, you are not simply asking for clarification—you are testing whether power is shared or guarded. And when the system is built on guarded power, rage becomes the defence that restores order.

This is why the reaction can feel irrational. Your question is proportionate. Your tone is calm. Your intention is honest. You are not attacking, accusing, or escalating. You are asking to be met. But the response is sharp, contemptuous, punitive, or suddenly cold. That *disproportion* is not accidental. It is diagnostic.

That disproportion is the point. It tells you you have stopped speaking to a person's *mood* and started speaking to a person's *design*. You are no longer interacting with personality—you are touching **structure**. And structures that depend on dominance cannot answer questions that imply equality. They can only repel them.

Rage, here, is not about emotion spilling over. It is about control being threatened. It is about a system recognising that something dangerous has entered the space: your refusal to accept asymmetry as normal. Rage is deployed to reassert hierarchy, to punish the question, to teach the body that fairness has consequences.

And once you see that, the reaction stops being confusing. It becomes legible. Not as passion. Not as pain. But as a **system protecting itself**.

Rage appears where hierarchy is exposed

Equality as a Threat

Equality removes the advantage on which control depends. Equality insists that both realities count, that both futures matter, that risk is shared, that consent is required, and that authority is mutual. It introduces symmetry into a system designed to operate through imbalance. It demands reciprocity where asymmetry once guaranteed comfort.

But in a hierarchy, one person's comfort sits above the other person's agency. Another person's accommodation preserves one person's ease.

Another person's flexibility stabilises one person's certainty. And that arrangement does not survive scrutiny. It cannot withstand sustained attention, because it relies on being treated as *natural* rather than *constructed.*

So when you bring equality into the relationship—through negotiation, through questions, through boundaries—you are not "making things difficult". You are not creating conflict. You are not introducing drama. You are interrupting the mechanism that makes the relationship workable for them. You are touching the operating system, not the surface behaviour.

Equality forces exposure. It forces the controlling partner to answer questions they were never intending to answer—questions the structure itself was designed to avoid. Questions that turn comfort into accountability and privilege into responsibility. Questions such as:

- Who carries the risk if things go wrong?
- Who benefits if things go right?
- Who is protected?
- Who is expendable?
- Who adjusts—and who is adjusted to?

These questions convert comfort into accountability.

These are not abstract questions. They are structural ones. And when those answers become visible—when the pattern can no longer hide behind intention, charm, or narrative—the illusion collapses. The story of mutuality can no longer hold. The imbalance can no longer be treated as accidental.

That collapse is experienced internally as a threat, even if you have done nothing threatening. Not because you are unsafe. Not because you are unreasonable. But because you are **uncontrollable**. And uncontrollability is intolerable to any system that depends on hierarchy to survive.

What feels like resistance is often grief for lost privilege.

Mutuality as Loss of Advantage

Mutuality is costly to someone who has been living on asymmetry. Mutuality requires: *accountability; reciprocity; shared decision-making; emotional exposure; structural fairness; limitation.* Each of these asks for something that asymmetry quietly removed. Each of these introduces friction into a system that depended on one-sided ease.

But a control-based identity experiences limitation as deprivation—not in the normal human sense, where two people negotiate needs and accept constraints as part of a relationship, but in the hierarchical sense, where access has been treated as an entitlement. Where preference has been mistaken for right, where being deferred to has been internalised as proof of worth.

In such systems, mutuality is not felt as balance. It is felt as a loss. Not loss of love, but loss of position. Loss of unchallenged authority. Loss of the ability to decide without consultation, to benefit without disclosure, to move without consequence.

So when you ask for mutuality, it registers as theft. Not because you are taking something that belongs to you—but because you are reclaiming something they were never meant to hold alone.

This is why fairness provokes such a peculiar kind of hostility. Because the controlling person is not hearing, *"Let's be equal."* They are hearing, *"You no longer have unilateral access."* They are hearing the end of special status, the end of exemption, the end of a structure that quietly centred their comfort as the organising principle.

They are hearing the end of their advantage.
And advantage is rarely surrendered politely. It is defended.

Reason threatens hierarchy because it requires reciprocity.

Why Rage Appears Instead of Reason

Because reason would require acknowledgement, and acknowledgement would require surrender. Surrender of position. Surrender of exemption. Surrender of the unspoken agreement that one reality matters more than the other.

Rage does not have to answer you. Rage only has to destabilise you. It only has to interrupt your steadiness, fracture your clarity, and make the cost of speaking feel higher than the cost of silence.

That is what rage does in these systems: it functions as a corrective force. It is not primarily about expression. It is about enforcement. It is the system reaching for the fastest available tool to restore imbalance when equilibrium threatens to take hold.

Rage achieves three things quickly. *It makes equality feel expensive.* If every fair question triggers a consequence, you learn to stop asking—not because the question was wrong, but because the punishment trains restraint. *It makes you doubt your right to speak.* You start monitoring your tone, your words, your timing. You start negotiating your own perception, rehearsing before you speak, editing before you feel. *It reasserts hierarchy without argument* because fear and fatigue do what persuasion cannot. Because exhaustion is more efficient than explanation.

Rage is not communication. It is correction.

Rage also serves a quieter purpose: it reframes the problem. The issue is no longer the structure you questioned, but the disruption you caused. The focus shifts from fairness to fallout, from content to consequence. You become the instability that must be managed.

This is why rage often arrives exactly when you are calm. Your calm is the threat. Your clarity is the threat. Your lack of panic means you are not governable through emotional leverage. You are not scrambling. You are not appeasing. You are seeing.

So the system escalates. Not to communicate. To re-establish position.

Some Systems Require Hierarchy to Function

This is the part many people do not want to accept: some relationships are not failing because of poor communication. They are failing because the relationship is operating exactly as designed. The distress you feel is not evidence of misunderstanding; it is evidence of accuracy. The system is not broken. It is *working*—just not for you.

A hierarchy-based relationship needs far more than dominance to survive. It requires structural asymmetry, repeated daily, and quietly defended as "normal." It needs:

- One person to absorb uncertainty
- One person to carry the emotional labour
- One person to adjust more
- One person to be more "understanding"
- One person to be more "flexible"
- One person to accept less protection while offering more provisions.

These are not incidental traits. They are functional requirements. Remove any one of them, and the system begins to destabilise. That system does not improve through conversation. Conversation threatens it. Because conversation introduces **shared reality**. And shared reality is incompatible with domination. Where reality is shared, power must be justified. Where power must be justified, hierarchy begins to collapse.

So the moment you insist on fairness, you trigger a defence response—not because your request is wrong, but because your request makes the arrangement impossible to maintain without force. Fairness removes the camouflage. It exposes the cost distribution. It reveals who benefits, who pays, and who has been trained to call that payment "love," "loyalty," or "being reasonable."

This is why rage often appears as soon as you touch structure, not behaviour, not tone, not timing, but structure itself:

- When you ask for clarity around risk
- When you ask for mutual protection
- When you name double standards
- When you resist, "that's just how it is"

- When you do not accept moral framing as a substitute for fairness

At this point, you are not arguing about details. You are challenging the organising principle. You are no longer negotiating within the system; you are questioning why the system exists. And systems built on hierarchy do not respond to that question with curiosity. They respond with **rage**, **withdrawal**, or **punishment**, because without hierarchy, they cannot function—and they know it.

At this point, behaviour no longer needs interpretation.

What Rage Is Really Saying

Rage is saying: *Stop bringing equality into a system that requires hierarchy.* Stop asking questions that restore your agency. Stop insisting on mutuality when the benefit depends on imbalance. What it is really defending is not order, not harmony, not stability, but **advantage**—an advantage that can only survive if it remains unnamed and unexamined.

Rage is the system snapping shut. Not because you raised your voice—but because you refused to disappear quietly. Because silence was part of the contract, and your awareness voided it. Because presence, once claimed, cannot be easily revoked without consequence.

And once you understand that, you understand something else: the rage is not evidence that you are wrong. It is evidence that you have touched the truth. You have reached the load-bearing wall. You have pressed against the place where justification ends, and coercion begins.

Because when someone wants partnership, fairness is relief. It reduces fear. It distributes responsibility. It makes intimacy possible. When someone wants dominance, fairness is *humiliation*. It exposes dependence on asymmetry. It reveals that power was never moral—it was merely *uncontested*.

And humiliation, in control-based systems, does not elicit reflection. It produces **retaliation**. It produces reassertion. It produces the urgent need to re-establish distance, superiority, or fear.

Which is why the next move is rarely discussion. It is *punishment*.

✦ When Structure Replaces Affection ✦

Contracts disguised as love • Why systems appear when care fails • How inevitability replaces intimacy

When affection fails, structure arrives. After rage, many people expect rupture—a break, a blow-up, a clear ending. However, what often follows is colder. Structure. Not the visible violence of collapse, but the quiet enforcement of continuity. Not chaos, but order imposed from above.

Not structure as maturity. Structure as control's second language—used when charm has failed, when silence no longer recalibrates, when negotiation has exposed the architecture, and rage has done its work. Structure appears precisely when the system has been named and can no longer rely on ambiguity. It is what replaces emotional leverage when it loses effectiveness.

Because rage is loud, structure is lasting. Rage disciplines the moment. Structure disciplines the future. Rage shocks the nervous system; structure reshapes the environment. Rage teaches you fear. Structure teaches you inevitability. Rage burns hot and briefly; structure settles in and governs.

And once a dynamic moves from affection to structure, it is no longer asking for love. It is asking for compliance—**efficiently**, **quietly**, with paperwork. With rules that sound reasonable. With procedures that appear neutral. With consequences that are framed as policy rather than choice. What was once relational becomes administrative. What was once emotional becomes procedural. And what was once requested freely is now imposed as an obligation.

This is how control stabilises itself. Not through intensity, but through permanence. Not through anger, but through design.

When love can no longer persuade, policy is introduced.

1. Contracts Disguised as Love

This is where many people get confused, because the language still sounds virtuous. It sounds responsible. It sounds adult. It sounds like care wearing a sensible coat:

"I'm just being practical."
"We need to be wise."
"This is how grown-ups do it."
"I'm protecting what I've built."
"Let's put things in place."

Each sentence gestures toward maturity, foresight, and stability. Each one borrows the moral authority of reason. But wisdom can be weaponised. Prudence can be selectively applied. And responsibility, when asymmetrical, becomes a mechanism of control rather than care.

In mutual relationships, structure protects both people. It acknowledges shared risk, distributes weight, and allows love to remain soft because safety is held by design. Structure here is not a cage but a scaffold. It exists to *support* intimacy, not replace it. It is transparent, revisable, and responsive to both parties' vulnerability.

In control-based relationships, structure is introduced for one purpose: **to make imbalance permanent**. What is framed as stability is, in fact, foreclosure. What is described as protection is the allocation of risk downward and benefit upward.

It turns advantage into policy. What was once implied becomes formalised. What was once tested becomes installed. What was once emotional becomes procedural. Power no longer needs to persuade once it has been written in. Consent is no longer requested once it has been assumed.

This is why the structure often feels oddly detailed in the places that affect you—and oddly vague in the places that protect you. Clauses are precise where your flexibility is required, and ambiguous where your safety would need definition. Obligations are explicit; care is implied. Enforcement is clear; accountability is theoretical.

You are given terms. Not tenderness.

Systems appear where responsiveness would have been required.

2. Why Systems Appear When Care Fails

Care is responsive. Care is relational. Care adjusts when reality changes. It listens for nuance. It remains permeable to new information. It responds to discomfort not as a threat, but as data. Care requires presence, flexibility, and the willingness to be affected.

A system does not need to care. A system only needs to function. It does not attune; it enforces. It does not listen; it executes. It does not adapt to the interior world; it prioritises outcomes. A system measures success by continuity rather than by well-being.

When affection is genuine, a partner remains curious when you are uneasy. They try to understand the shape of your concern. They do not punish questions; they answer them. They do not treat your autonomy as rebellion; they integrate it. Your subjectivity is not an obstacle—it is part of the relationship's intelligence.

But when care is missing—or when care was never the goal—systems appear. Not accidentally. Not prematurely. Precisely when responsiveness would be required, and cannot be offered.

Because systems do what empathy would have had to do: stabilise outcomes, reduce negotiation, remove your leverage, and make your consent less relevant over time. They convert relational uncertainty into procedural certainty. They replace *listening* with *rules. Structure replaces tenderness when tenderness cannot survive equality.*

And notice what happens at this stage: the relationship becomes less about who you are and more about what role you will accept. Identity gives way to function. Presence is exchanged for compliance. You are no longer encountered; you are positioned.

Your interior life becomes inconvenient. Your needs become "complications." Your questions become "resistance." Language shifts subtly, but decisively—from relational to managerial, from intimate to administrative.

Not because you are asking for too much, but because the system cannot afford responsiveness. Responsiveness would require ongoing adjustment. It would require power to move. It would require the sharing of risk.

Responsiveness would require mutuality. And mutuality would dismantle the arrangement.

So the system comes instead.

This is where choice quietly disappears.

3. How Inevitability Replaces Intimacy

One of the most chilling shifts in these dynamics is not anger. It is **inevitability**. Not heat, not explosion, not visible conflict—but the slow settling of certainty, the sense that something has closed before it was ever openly discussed. Inevitability carries no noise. It arrives quietly and rearranges the emotional landscape without asking permission.

The feeling that the future has already been decided, and your job is to adjust your emotions to match it. Not to participate, not to co-create, not to question—but to *adapt*. To align your inner world with an external plan that is already moving forward without you.

This is how inevitability enters:
decisions are presented as conclusions, not conversations;
terms are framed as "reality", and your discomfort as immaturity;
the future is spoken of as settled, while your consent is treated as

formality;
pushback is met with moral language: "Then don't marry." "You're not ready." "This is what marriage is."

Each move narrows the field. Each phrase closes a door. What looks like pragmatism is actually compression—of choice, of voice, of possibility. **Inevitability is power disguised as practicality.** It is how a person stops persuading you and starts positioning you. It is how agency is replaced with adjustment.

And this is the moment many women finally understand what has been happening. Not all at once, but with a quiet, devastating clarity that cannot be unseen:

The relationship was not moving toward partnership. It was moving toward **infrastructure**. Toward permanence without reciprocity. Toward stability without intimacy.

You were not being loved into a future. You were being installed into one. Slot by slot. Expectation by expectation. Until your presence was assumed rather than welcomed.

This is why intimacy begins to die here. Because intimacy requires uncertainty, it requires vulnerability. It requires the willingness to be shaped by another person's reality. It requires openness to change—not only in feelings but also in outcomes.

A system cannot be shaped. It can only be accepted—or resisted. It does not bend toward you. It waits for you to comply.

And the moment you resist, the truth becomes unmistakable: **you are**

not negotiating a relationship. You are negotiating your place inside someone else's design.

The Signature Tells

When structure replaces affection, certain tells appear—quiet, repeatable, diagnostic. They do not arrive as explosions. They arrive as patterns. Small shifts that repeat often enough to become the climate. These tells are not dramatic. They are diagnostic:

- Warmth becomes conditional on compliance
- Kindness appears when you yield and disappears when you question
- "Love" is spoken, but care is procedural
- Your labour is assumed, but your protection is debated
- You feel managed, not met
- You start preparing sentences the way people prepare defences

None of these moments, taken alone, seems decisive. That is part of their power. Each can be explained away. Each can be rationalised as stress, pragmatism, maturity, or timing. But together they form a signature—a coherent logic that reveals itself only through accumulation. What you are experiencing is not inconsistency. It is *consistency of a different kind.*

And then one day, you notice something that ends the fantasy. Not dramatically. Not all at once. But with a clarity that rearranges everything you thought you understood:

You are doing relational work in a relational environment that no longer behaves relationally.

You are offering presence, curiosity, care, and emotional risk. You are adjusting, attuning, explaining, softening. You are speaking like a person. **The structure is responding like a system,** not listening, not meeting, not changing—only processing, categorising, enforcing.

Once you see that, you cannot unsee it, because systems do not misunderstand you. They *replace* you. They do not fail to love; they were never designed to.

What This Chapter Is Really Naming

This chapter is not about contracts. Contracts can be wise. This chapter is about contracts used to replace **conscience**—about what happens when written terms are asked to do the moral work that a human being will not do themselves.

Because when conscience is present, structure is fair. It is responsive. It bends when reality bends. It protects without erasing. When conscience is absent, structure is **strategy**. It is no longer there to support a relationship; it is there to *manage exposure*, to distribute cost, to lock in an advantage while appearing reasonable.

And strategy has a specific goal: **to remove the need for love**.

Love is unpredictable. Love listens. Love has to consider you. Love requires ongoing engagement with another person's interior life. Love cannot be finalised, formalised, or fixed in advance without ceasing to be love.

A system does not. A system only needs you to comply.

This is where many readers recognise their own story.

The Moment You (the Reader) Should Not Miss

If you are reading this and you recognise the shift from affection to structure, note this carefully, because it is the hinge on which everything turns:

When someone stops trying to be close to you and starts trying to secure outcomes from you, the relationship has already changed categories. Quietly. Irreversibly. What was once relational has become operational.

That is not "adulting." That is not "realism." That is not "leadership." Those are labels used to make inevitability sound virtuous and compliance sound mature.

That is the point where **intimacy is replaced with inevitability**.

And once inevitability enters, the question is no longer: *"Do they love me?"*
The question becomes: *"What am I being positioned to absorb?"*

Because in these systems, structure is never neutral. Structure is never merely practical. Structure is **the cage with polite language**—the mechanism that ensures the cost continues to flow in one direction while appearing orderly, rational, and fair.

And when affection is replaced by structure, what is offered is not partnership. It is not mutuality. It is not shared risk.

It is **containment**.

By now, the pattern is visible. Not because it is dramatic, but because it is consistent. What began as a connection became leverage. What felt like silence became calibration. What sounded like negotiation became a threat. What followed fairness was rage. And what replaced affection was structure.

None of this required cruelty to begin. None of it required conscious malice. It required only one thing: **a system that could not tolerate equality**.

Part II has traced how control operates—step by step, without pathology, without villainy. Not as personality, but as **design**. Not as emotion, but as a **mechanism**. Not as a failure of love, but as a substitution for it.

But mechanisms do not exist without belief.

No one sustains dominance accidentally. No one maintains hierarchy without a story that makes it feel necessary, justified, or virtuous. Power always carries a narrative that tells itself it is reasonable.

The next question is not what they do.
It is **why it feels right to them to do it**.

III

✦ THE ILLUSION OF SAFETY ✦

Why control masquerades as care

Control rarely presents itself as control. It presents as safety.
As certainty. As leadership, protection, foresight.
It promises order in a world that feels unstable
and relief from the burden of uncertainty.

This is how dominance learns to sound like care.
Part III examines the beliefs that make control feel
responsible,
hierarchy feel necessary, and equality feel dangerous—
revealing why some people mistake being governed
for being protecte

✦ When Control Feels Like Security ✦

Why some people equate dominance with stability
· Why uncertainty is intolerable to them

Control rarely introduces itself as control. It introduces itself as **stability**. As **order**. As **wisdom**. As **protection from chaos**. It does not arrive with threat or volatility. It arrives composed. Measured. Reasonable. It speaks in calm sentences and practical tones, borrowing the language of care to mask the logic of command.

It calls its preferences "standards" and its demands "structure". It frames limitation as maturity and constraint as foresight. It makes certainty sound like *love*. And because many people are hungry for safety—because uncertainty has already wounded them—this framing works. Not because they are foolish, but because they have learned, sometimes through real pain, that unpredictability can destroy you. Chaos costs—ambiguity exhausts. Instability hurts.

So when someone arrives offering certainty, the offer can feel like refuge. Like relief. Like a place to finally rest. It can feel like being held rather than managed, guided rather than governed.

But certainty is not always care. Sometimes it is **domination with good**

posture. Sometimes it is control standing very still, speaking very softly, and calling itself protection.

And that is what makes it so difficult to recognise, because it does not look like danger. It appears *safe*, until you realise whose safety it is designed to preserve.

This is how control becomes believable: it presents hierarchy as a form of relief.

Why Dominance Can Feel Like Stability

Stability is a real need. Most people do not want drama. They want predictability. They want to know where they stand. They want a home inside the relationship—a place where their nervous system can rest. This is not a weakness. It is biology. It is the human need for safety, continuity, and orientation.

A mutual partner builds that with **responsiveness**. Stability here is alive, relational, and shared. It is created moment by moment through engagement rather than enforcement:

- They listen
- They repair
- They adjust
- They share risk
- They stay human under pressure.

This kind of stability is flexible. It can tolerate uncertainty because responsibility is distributed. No one person has to hold all the control for the system to function.

A controlling partner builds a different kind of stability. Not one rooted in responsiveness, but one rooted in **closure**. This stability is achieved not by adapting to reality, but by narrowing it:

- They decide early
- They define terms
- They set roles
- They close questions
- They reduce variables

And here is the seduction: **this can feel calm—especially at first**. Because when one person insists on being the centre of decision-making, the relationship becomes more predictable. Fewer negotiations. Fewer unknowns. Fewer open ends. Not more loving—*more predictable*. The system runs smoothly, as long as the other person cooperates. As long as friction is avoided. As long as differences do not surface.

So dominance can masquerade as **leadership**.
Control can masquerade as **maturity**.
Restriction can masquerade as **responsibility**.

It is not the words that signal danger. It is what becomes non-negotiable underneath them.

It sounds like:
"I'm just thinking ahead."
"I'm trying to protect us."
"This is how it has to be."
"I know what works."
"I don't want confusion."

To someone who fears instability, these sentences feel like shelter. They promise order. They promise certainty. They promise relief from the exhausting work of negotiation and uncertainty.

But shelter that requires your shrinking is not safety. It is management. And what is being stabilised is not the relationship but the hierarchy within it.

That is why dominance can feel so convincing at first. It does not announce itself as power. It announces itself as *peace.*

The Hidden Bargain Beneath 'Security'

When control feels like security, there is usually an unspoken bargain underneath it. It is rarely announced. It is never negotiated openly. It is assumed, embedded in tone, expectation, and consequence:

I will reduce uncertainty for you—if you reduce yourself for me.

That is the exchange. Clean. Asymmetrical. Efficient.

You get the comfort of answers, direction, and firmness. You get relief from ambiguity. You get the sense that someone else is holding the map, setting the pace, deciding what matters. For a nervous system exhausted by instability, this can feel like being carried.

In return, you surrender a quiet set of freedoms—not all at once, not dramatically, but incrementally, until the cost becomes structural:

- the freedom to question without consequence
- the freedom to change your mind without punishment

- the freedom to be complex without being corrected
- the freedom to disagree without being framed as disloyal
- the freedom to have needs without being labelled difficult

None of these freedoms is taken explicitly. They are *priced*. Each time you exercise one, something subtle is withdrawn—warmth, patience, goodwill, ease. Over time, the lesson becomes embodied: some parts of you are too expensive to express.

This is why some controlling relationships feel "peaceful" on the outside. There are fewer arguments. Fewer surprises. Fewer visible conflicts. The surface is calm because the variables have been reduced.

But peace has been purchased. And the currency is **agency**.
And what you pay for most is not comfort. It is a voice.

What appears to be safety is often merely silence purchased at a high internal cost. What feels like security is frequently containment that has learned how to speak gently.

Why Uncertainty Is Intolerable to Them

Uncertainty is not just discomfort to some people. They are not stabilised by connection; they are stabilised by control. It is a **threat**—not because they are evil, but because they are organised around control as a survival strategy. Control is not merely a preference for them; it is how their inner world stays coherent. Their emotional architecture cannot tolerate open-endedness, mutual influence, or shared decision-making without perceiving them as sources of instability. What feels like flexibility to another person feels like danger here.

Uncertainty requires:

- Trust in another person's autonomy
- Willingness to be affected
- Capacity to not win
- Ability to be wrong
- Ability to negotiate without losing identity

Each of these requires a stable sense of self that does not depend on dominance. A control-based identity experiences these not as skills, but as **exposure**. To be affected feels like a loss. To not win feels like erasure. To be wrong feels like a collapse. Instead of addressing uncertainty, they seek to eliminate it.

They manage outcomes. They pre-decide the future. They prefer roles to relationships—because roles reduce risk. Roles remove ambiguity. Roles make behaviour legible in advance.

Roles tell you who speaks, who follows, who adjusts, who carries, and who sacrifices. Roles assign weight before reality arrives. Roles make life predictable. And predictability can feel like safety to someone who cannot emotionally tolerate mutuality.

But what they call "uncertainty" is often just **shared humanity**.

Your autonomy is "uncertainty".
Your needs are "complications".
Your questions are "instability".
Your boundaries are "problems".

Not because those things are wrong—but because they cannot be controlled.

How This Shows Up in Real Time

When control feels like security, you will notice an emotional pattern. It does not announce itself dramatically. It reveals itself through conditions.

Closeness is allowed—until you introduce **choice**.

As long as you are aligned, the system feels calm. There is ease. There is flow. There is reassurance. But the calm is contingent. When you ask a question, slow the pace, request reciprocity, or insist on mutual protection, something changes—not always in volume, sometimes in *temperature*. The shift is subtle but unmistakable:
The system stays calm until you reintroduce choice.

- Warmth becomes thin
- Patience becomes performative
- "Discussion" becomes correction
- Your concerns become your flaws
- Your hesitation becomes disrespect

Each change signals the same thing: you have crossed an invisible line. Not a boundary of behaviour, but a boundary of *power*.

Because your agency reintroduces uncertainty—and uncertainty is what they are trying to remove. Your choice destabilises what was meant to remain settled. Your voice interrupts what was intended to proceed uninterrupted.

This is why many people say, "He was wonderful until I needed something." Or, "She was calm until I disagreed." These statements are not contradictions; they are diagnoses.

What they mean is: the calmness was **conditional**—not on love, but on *compliance.*

The Difference Between Safety and Control

This is the clean distinction. Not a subtle one. Not a philosophical one. A functional one that the body understands immediately, even when the mind hesitates:

Safety can tolerate your no. Control cannot.

Safety does not require you to disappear to keep the peace. It does not rely on your silence to maintain stability. Safety does not punish reality. It does not demand emotional distortion or self-erasure as the price of harmony. Safety does not require certainty as proof of love. It allows hesitation, complexity, and change. Safety can hold two minds, two needs, two futures in the same room without treating difference as danger.

Control wants one mind. One plan. One authority.

Not because that is healthier, but because it is simpler. Because one authority is easier to stabilise than two equal humans. One voice is easier to manage than dialogue. One will is easier to protect than shared power.

Control does not fail because of conflict. It fails because of **plurality**. It collapses when reality refuses to be singular.

So, if a person repeatedly treats mutuality as disorder, experiences your autonomy as disruption, and your equality as instability, what they are seeking is not partnership. They are seeking **relief**—relief from negotiation, from influence, from the responsibility of being shaped by another person.

They are seeking relief from having to share power.
And that is the difference that decides everything.

The Quiet Warning Inside 'Security'

Many people remain too long because control does not always feel dangerous. Sometimes it feels like finally being held by something firm—something decisive, something that promises not to waver. After chaos, uncertainty, or emotional exhaustion, firmness can feel like a form of relief. It can feel like safety.

But firmness without tenderness is not stability. It is a cage that doesn't rattle. It does not clang or alarm. It simply closes, quietly, around whatever no longer moves.

And the moment to pay attention is not when the person becomes loud. It is not when they shout, threaten, or overtly dominate. It is when they become **certain** in a way that leaves no room for you, when the future is spoken of as finished, when disagreement is treated as confusion, when your presence is tolerated only if it does not alter the outcome.

Because in healthy intimacy, certainty has **softness**. It can change. It can listen. It can revise. It can be wrong. It knows that being sure does not require being fixed. It leaves space for another mind to matter.

In control, certainty becomes a **weapon**. It does not persuade. It concludes. It ends the discussion before it begins. It replaces curiosity with finality and calls that strength.

And once a relationship is built on conclusions rather than connection, the future is not being shared. It is no longer something you are walking into together.

It is being **assigned**.

That is not security.
That is submission, renamed.

✦ Decline and the Hunger for Governable Partners ✦

Ageing, illness, relevance anxiety • Why dependency is outsourced • Why autonomy becomes threatening

Decline changes the body. It changes time. It changes leverage. What once felt abundant begins to feel finite. What once could be deferred now presses forward. The future contracts, and with them, tolerance for uncertainty.

For some people, decline also changes the kind of partner they seek—not towards love, but towards **management**. Not towards intimacy, but towards **insurance**. Not towards mutuality, but towards someone governable enough to absorb what life is beginning to take from them. Someone adjustable. Someone reliable in asymmetry. Someone whose needs can be postponed so their own can be prioritised without negotiation.

This is not always conscious. It is not always articulated. But it is often **consistent**. Patterns emerge not through intention, but through repetition. What is chosen repeatedly reveals what is required.

When a person is organised around control, decline does not soften them. It tightens them. It sharpens the need for predictability. It increases the urgency to stabilise outcomes. Because decline introduces the one thing they cannot tolerate: **dependence they cannot command**. Dependence that cannot be scheduled, limited, or framed as generosity.

So they try to command it.
They substitute care with control.
They replace intimacy with governance.
They seek not a partner, but a system that will hold when they can no longer bend.

And this is where love is most at risk—not because decline is inherently corrupting, but because fear, when paired with power, seeks certainty at any cost.

Decline does not create control. It reveals how control has been used to foster a sense of safety.

Ageing, Illness, and Relevance Anxiety

Decline is not only physical. It is **existential**. It does not merely affect capacity; it confronts identity. It brings a person face-to-face with realities that cannot be optimised away or reframed as a matter of preference. It confronts a person with:

- limits they cannot negotiate
- a future they cannot fully plan
- a body that will not obey
- a world that is moving on without asking their permission

These encounters destabilise the stories people tell themselves about who they are and what guarantees them value. They expose the difference between competence and worth, between usefulness and dignity.

For a mutual person, this can produce humility, grief, reorientation, and a more profound tenderness for what matters. It can widen empathy. It can soften defences. It can recalibrate power into care and presence. Decline, here, becomes an invitation to intimacy rather than a threat to identity.

For a control-based identity, decline can feel like *humiliation*—because their self-concept has often been built on being:

- the one who provides
- the one who decides
- the one who is needed
- the one who is "above" specific vulnerabilities

Decline removes that posture. It strips away the distance that power once created. It makes them ordinary. It makes them mortal. It makes them subject to forces they cannot dominate—time, dependence, and irreversibility.

When a person cannot tolerate being reachable, they seek a substitute. Not for care, but for control. Not for mutual holding, but for leverage.

They look for a person they can **govern**.
Governance becomes a substitute for the authority decline has removed.

Not because they want to harm—but because governing another person restores the illusion of relevance, authority, and immunity that decline has taken away. It is an attempt to relocate power externally when it can no longer be sustained internally.

And this is where fear quietly reshapes love into management.

Why Dependency Gets Outsourced

Here is the quiet truth: ***some people do not want a partner. They want a stabiliser.*** Someone whose presence reduces volatility, absorbs uncertainty, and makes life feel more manageable without requiring reciprocal vulnerability.

Decline forces practical needs into the open. Needs that can no longer be postponed, disguised, or outsourced to circumstance alone:

- care
- monitoring
- reminders
- support
- emotional regulation
- logistics
- crisis management

These needs are not shameful. They are human. They are what emerge when life becomes less forgiving and more complex.

In a healthy bond, these needs are held **together**. They are spoken plainly, negotiated fairly, and reciprocated over time. Care remains relational. It moves both ways. It is responsive rather than extracted. No one person becomes the permanent container for the other's fear.

But in a control-based dynamic, dependency is treated like a **threat to status**. Needing help feels like a loss of position. Vulnerability feels like exposure. So instead of saying, *I'm scared*, they build an arrangement that makes someone else responsible for that fear. Instead of admitting that *I need help*, they create a role in which help becomes a **duty**. Instead of asking, *Will you be with me through hard seasons?*, they frame it as: "If you're mine, you must."

This is how dependency gets outsourced: the vulnerability is never shared. It is **assigned**.
What is assigned cannot be refused without consequence.

And because it is assigned rather than mutually held, the person doing the caring begins to feel it—not all at once, but unmistakably, in the body and in the tone of the relationship:

- as an obligation, not love
- as pressure, not devotion
- as responsibility without protection

Care stops feeling chosen. It starts feeling required. What once might have been intimacy becomes maintenance.

The relationship becomes less like companionship and more like **unpaid labour with romantic language**.

And this is the final shift to notice: love is no longer something that happens *between* two people. It becomes something extracted *from* one person to stabilise another.

Why Autonomy Becomes Threatening

Autonomy is tolerated only when it does not disrupt the system. Autonomy is acceptable only when it remains decorative. As long as independence exists at the margins—so long as it does not alter outcomes, timelines, or authority—it can be praised, even admired. But decline makes the system **fragile**. What once felt manageable begins to feel exposed. What once could be absorbed now feels like risk.

When someone is ageing, unwell, or frightened of losing relevance, they often become acutely sensitive to anything that implies:

- You might not be there
- You might choose yourself
- You might require fairness
- You might leave
- You might see clearly

Each implication threatens more than the relationship. It endangers the scaffolding holding their future together. It threatens the assumption of availability, loyalty, and access that has quietly stabilised them.

So, autonomy becomes less attractive and more **dangerous**. Because autonomy introduces uncertainty, and uncertainty, to a control-based identity in decline, feels like abandonment *before it happens*. It feels like a loss arriving early. It feels like standing unprotected at the edge of time.

This is why they often escalate around:

- commitment

- marriage
- caregiving roles
- financial terms
- access to your time and body
- being named as "next of kin"
- being positioned as the default contact, responder, safety net

These are not random pressure points. They are structural anchors. Each one secures proximity, obligation, and future access. Each one reduces the chance that your autonomy could later disrupt what is being silently relied upon.

Not always with overt force. Sometimes with righteousness. Sometimes with "wisdom". Sometimes with spiritual framing. Sometimes with language that sounds like destiny, duty, or maturity. But the goal is the same: **to make your freedom feel like betrayal**.

Because if your freedom remains intact, their future remains uncertain—and they cannot tolerate that.

So autonomy must be reframed. Not as growth. Not as healthy. But as selfishness. As fear. As immaturity. As a failure to commit. As a lack of love.

And that is the final inversion to recognise: your independence is not threatening because it is wrong, but because it is real.

The Most Dangerous Contradiction

In these dynamics, the person may simultaneously require you as a **lifeline** and distrust you as a **risk**. These two positions do not alternate; they coexist. They are held simultaneously, producing a tension that never resolves because it is not intended to. Dependence increases fear. Fear increases control.

They want your care without your agency. They want your loyalty without your **leverage**. What is being sought is not a relationship, but access—access that cannot be interrupted by choice.

So they create an atmosphere where you are not simply loved or needed, but positioned:

- essential, but suspected
- needed, but monitored
- recruited, but never fully trusted

You are close, but never safe. Valued, but never autonomous. The closeness is conditional, and the suspicion is permanent.

This is why you can see two messages at once. They are not contradictions to the system; they *are* the system:

"I need you."
"And I will control you so you cannot become dangerous to me."

Care is demanded, but freedom is constrained. Attachment is encouraged, but independence is policed. The relationship tightens precisely where trust should deepen.

Because in their internal logic, your autonomy is the only threat that matters—not because you are unsafe, not because you are unreliable, but because you are **free**. And freedom introduces the one possibility they cannot manage: that you might choose differently.

That is the contradiction at the centre of control-based bonds. And it is why love, no matter how sincerely spoken, is never allowed to exist without supervision.

A Clean Diagnostic

When decline is present, love has a particular shape. It does not harden. It does not rush to secure an advantage. Love gets **humbler**, **softer**, more honest. It loosens its grip on certainty. It makes room for fear without reducing it to authority. It allows vulnerability to be recognised without reducing it to entitlement.

Love under pressure does not ask for obedience. It asks for presence. It does not reduce the other person to feel safe. It allows both people to remain human, uncertain, and intact.

Control has a different shape. Control does not soften under strain—it **tightens**. It becomes more urgent, more positional, more transactional. It seeks guarantees instead of connection. It treats care like a **contract** and commitment like a **cage**. What it cannot tolerate emotionally, it tries to stabilise structurally.

So the diagnosis is this. It is simple, but it is decisive:

Does their vulnerability make them more mutual—or more entitled?

A mutual person states, "This is hard." Let's face it together.
A control-based person says, "This is hard". So you must become mine.

That single distinction tells you everything. It tells you whether fear is being shared—or leveraged. Whether closeness is being invited or enforced. Whether love is expanding to meet reality—or shrinking reality to preserve power.

And once you see that distinction clearly, you cannot unsee it.

Closing: The Hunger for the Governable

Decline does not automatically corrupt a person. But it exposes what has been underneath. It removes the buffers that once hid motive inside momentum. It strips away surplus and reveals structure. Under pressure, what is essential surfaces.

If someone has built their identity on dominance, decline feels like a loss of self. Not inconvenient. Not adjustment. *Loss.* The loss of position, relevance, authority, and the illusion of invulnerability. And rather than grieve honestly—rather than allow that loss to transform them—they attempt to preserve themselves by installing someone else as **support infrastructure**. Another human becomes a load-bearing beam.

This is the hunger for governable partners. Not a hunger for love, but a hunger for **certainty**. A hunger for access that cannot leave. A hunger for a person who will absorb the future for them—who will hold risk, manage fear, stabilise outcomes, and remain available regardless of cost. What is being sought is not intimacy, but insulation.

And the moment you insist on being an equal human—an equal soul with choice—your equality reintroduces the very thing they were trying to escape: **uncertainty**. Choice destabilises what was meant to remain guaranteed. Agency interrupts what was meant to be secured.

Which is why autonomy becomes threatening—not because you are wrong, not because you are cruel, not because you are abandoning them—but because you are **real**. Real people cannot be guaranteed. Real people cannot be governed without cost. Real people bring uncertainty simply by remaining themselves.

And that is the truth this chapter leaves you with:
what they fear is not your leaving, but your freedom to leave.

✦ When Care Becomes a Liability ✦

Why nurturing partners are targeted • Why generosity invites extraction • Why goodness is misread as availability

Care is supposed to be a strength. Empathy. Generosity. Attunement. The ability to notice another person's needs and respond without being asked. These capacities are not incidental to love; they are its infrastructure. In healthy relationships, these qualities deepen trust, create safety, and allow intimacy to grow. They move freely because they are met, reciprocated, and protected.

But in control-based dynamics, care does something else. It attracts **extraction**. Not admiration. Not protection. Not reverence. Use.

Not because care is weak—but because it is **usable**. It is reliable. It shows up. It fills gaps. It stabilises chaos. It absorbs impact. It keeps things running. And systems organised around control notice exactly these properties.

Care is not dangerous in itself. But in control-based systems, care becomes useful. Not cherished. Not protected. **Used**. It becomes a resource rather than a gift. Something that can be drawn upon repeatedly without replenishment, because it does not announce its limits loudly.

And this is where many people finally feel something turn upside down. The moral order they trusted begins to invert. The very qualities they believed would create safety—**kindness**, **patience**, **empathy**, **generosity**—start to work against them. Not because those qualities are flawed, not because they were given in error, but because they are **legible**. They are predictable. They can be relied upon without consent.

And legibility invites **extraction**.

Once care is read as dependable, it is no longer treated as precious. It is treated as available. Once availability is assumed, it is no longer thanked. It is scheduled. Expected. Required. What was once voluntary becomes structural.

This is the quiet betrayal inside control-based dynamics: care is not met with care. It is met with **demand**. And the more generously you give, the more the system learns that it does not need to give back.

Not because you gave too much—but because you were never meant to be protected in return.

Care does not fail here. The structure fails to honour it.

Why Nurturing Partners Are Targeted

Contrary to popular belief, controlling dynamics do not primarily target vulnerable individuals. ***They seek functional people.*** People who can hold weight without collapsing. People whose strength is quiet, steady, and reliable.

Control does not seek cruelty first. It seeks **capacity**. People who:

- anticipate needs
- tolerate discomfort without complaint
- prioritise harmony
- value commitment
- hold responsibility seriously
- stay emotionally present under strain

These qualities are often praised as virtues. And they are virtues in mutual systems. But in a system organised around control, these qualities become signals. They indicate reliability. Endurance. Adaptability. And reliability, in a control-based system becomes an **opportunity**.

A nurturing partner is appealing because they regulate environments. They smooth tension. They absorb volatility. They fill gaps without being told. They make life easier. They notice what others overlook and respond before issues escalate. And for someone who fears uncertainty, that ease is intoxicating. It feels like safety without vulnerability—stability without reciprocity.

So the attraction is not accidental. It is **strategic**—not always consciously, but consistently. Patterns do not require intent to be real. They only require repetition.

Because nurturing people do something powerful: they make dysfunction survivable. They make dysfunction look stable. They explain. They contextualise. They forgive. They try again. They hold complexity. They stay kind. They remain human under strain. They translate chaos into coherence and call it love.

And that makes them ideal targets. Not because they are weak—but because they are **capable**. Capable of carrying what was never meant to be carried alone.

A nurturing partner does not escalate easily. They explain. They contextualise. They forgive. They try again. This buys the system time: time to test boundaries, time to install expectations, time to convert care into **duty**. Time for what began as generosity to become an obligation.

By the time the nurturing partner realises what has happened, their strength has already been integrated into the structure. What once felt like love is now load-bearing.

And that is the danger no one warns them about:
their goodness does not protect them.
It makes them useful.

Why Generosity Invites Extraction

Generosity is often mistaken for resilience. When you give easily, some people assume you can give endlessly. When you forgive quickly, some people assume you will ignore everything. When you adapt without protest, some people assume adaptation is your role. What begins as a freely offered quality is quietly reframed as a permanent condition.

This is how generosity becomes reinterpreted—not as ***choice****, but as* ***capacity****.* Once something is recognised as a capacity, it is treated as a **resource**. It ceases to be something you *offer* and becomes something others feel entitled to *use*.

The first time you give freely, it is appreciated. The second time, it is expected. The third time, it is assumed. What once felt relational becomes procedural.

First, it is appreciated. Then it is normal. Then it is required. Extraction rarely begins with demand. It starts as an **assumption**—the soft, unchallenged belief that your giving is simply how things work:

"You'll understand."
"You won't mind."
"You're good at handling things."
"You're stronger than me."
"You're better with emotions."
"You're more flexible."

None of these statements sounds violent. None of them announces exploitation. They sound complementary. They sound grateful. But together, they build a system where your giving is no longer voluntary. It becomes expected. And **expectation is where generosity dies**.

What begins as gratitude quietly becomes entitlement.

Extraction rarely begins with theft. It starts with **entitlement disguised as need**. It sounds like:

"You know I'm going through a lot."
"You're the only one I can rely on."
"You're strong—you can handle it."
"This is what commitment looks like."

Each sentence quietly shifts responsibility. Each one relocates the burden without consent. Slowly, without being named, your giving becomes part of the **operating budget**. Not a gift. A requirement. Not a choice. A baseline.

And this is the devastation many generous people feel too late: what they gave in love is now treated as infrastructure. What once came from the heart is now expected by default. And the moment you hesitate, you are no longer seen as human—you are seen as *failing*.

That is the final inversion.
Generosity is not exhausted by giving.
It is exhausted by entitlement.

Why Goodness Is Misread as Availability

One of the most corrosive distortions in control-based dynamics is th**e interpretation of goodness as access**. What should signal discernment and care is instead read as openness without limit. What should invite respect is translated into permission.

Your kindness serves as evidence that you will stay. Your patience becomes proof that you will endure. Your empathy becomes proof that you will excuse. Your loyalty becomes proof that you will not leave. Because you do not weaponise your care, it is assumed that you will not withdraw it. The absence of threat is misread as the absence of boundaries.

This is the mistake.

A controlling system does not experience goodness as boundary-aware. It experiences goodness as *open*. It does not ask where your limits are; it assumes they are negotiable. Goodness is often mistaken for **consent**—not conscious consent, but **structural consent**: the belief that what you have given before will always be given again.

A kind person can be deeply discerning, but people who extract do not read nuance—they read **patterns**. And kindness can create a visible pattern: you forgive quickly, you explain yourself, you consider others' stress, you give second chances, you avoid being unfair, you avoid conflict, you keep your tone gentle. These behaviours are not weaknesses; they are signs of emotional literacy. But in a system organised around control, they are logged as predictability.

So when you later introduce limits—when you say *no*, slow down, ask for fairness, or protect yourself—the reaction is often shock, then punishment. Not because the boundary is unreasonable, not because your care was insincere, but because it contradicts the role you were assigned. The system was calibrated to your availability, not your agency.

You were not meant to choose care.
You were meant to be care.

Choice is what made your care dangerous to the system.

And that is the quiet theft at the centre of this distortion: your humanity is reduced to function. Your goodness is no longer something you offer; it is something others feel entitled to access. When you reclaim it as choice, the system experiences loss—and responds accordingly.

That is why goodness, when unprotected, becomes dangerous not to you, but **for you**.

When Virtue Is Turned Into Leverage

There is another layer to this distortion that is rarely named, especially in moral or religious contexts—one that operates quietly, often under the appearance of goodness, and therefore evades scrutiny. It does not look like cruelty. It looks like a principle.

For many people raised with strong values—faith, conscience, devotion, spiritual discipline—goodness is not just a preference. It is an identity. Love is taught as sacrifice. Forgiveness is framed as a virtue. Endurance is praised as holiness. Turning the other cheek is elevated above self-protection. And suffering quietly is often mistaken for moral depth. These teachings are rarely offered with malice; they are usually inherited with sincerity and reverence.

In these frameworks, harm is not always confronted—it is spiritualised. Pain is given meaning instead of limits. Endurance is sanctified rather than examined. Silence is rewarded rather than questioned.

This creates a dangerous vulnerability: virtue becomes detachable from agency. Goodness is preserved, but the person is not.

When love is taught as unlimited tolerance, harm gains a moral disguise. When forgiveness is emphasised without discernment, accountability disappears. When self-protection is framed as selfishness, boundaries begin to feel like betrayal—not of the relationship, but of one's own values. The person does not merely fear conflict; they fear becoming "bad".

And this is where goodness becomes exploitable.

People who know how to extract do not need to destroy your morals. They only need to reinterpret them. They quote your values back to you. They question your faith when you resist. They frame your limits as hardness, your withdrawal as unloving, your self-respect as pride. They suggest that if you were truly good, truly faithful, truly compassionate, you would endure more.

Your virtue is used as leverage.
"You're supposed to forgive."
"Love is patient."
"A good person wouldn't react this way."
"This isn't very Christian of you."
"If you were spiritually mature, you'd understand."

None of these statements addresses the harm. They bypass it. They shift the focus from impact to identity. The question quietly shifts from "*What is happening here?*" to *What kind of person are you being right now?* The harm becomes secondary. Your goodness becomes the terrain of control.

And that shift is not accidental.

When virtue is disconnected from the strength of character, it loses its anchor. It becomes weight-bearing without support. Goodness, without agency, has nothing to rest on. It cannot protect itself. It cannot say no without feeling immoral. It cannot leave without feeling like a failure. The very values meant to guide life begin to police it.

This is how morality becomes a mechanism of control.

The system does not need to convince you that harm is good. It only needs to convince you that resisting harm is bad. Once that inversion takes hold, your values no longer guard your dignity—they are used to override it. You become governable through your own conscience.

But virtue was never meant to function alone.

Strength of character is what allows goodness to remain voluntary. Discernment is what allows compassion to stay clean. Agency is what keeps love from turning into submission. Without these, virtue becomes a tool others can wield against you while calling it righteousness.

This is not a failure of faith. It is a misuse of it.

For some, anchoring comes through God—because God is not extractive. God does not require you to disappear to be holy. God does not confuse endurance with love or silence with virtue. A stable spiritual anchor does not demand that you tolerate harm to prove goodness. It gives you somewhere to stand when goodness is tested, somewhere that does not move when pressure is applied.

For others, the anchor may be conscience, integrity, deeply held principles, or a disciplined relationship with solitude and self-knowledge. The language differs, but the structure is the same: goodness must be supported by something that another person cannot negotiate away. Something that does not collapse when approval is withdrawn.

Because goodness without grounding is not strength, it is exposure.

And when virtue is stripped of its right to protect itself, it is no longer love. It is labour performed under moral threat.

That is how goodness is misread not just as availability, but as obligation.

The Silent Role Assignment

In these dynamics, nurturing partners are rarely asked to take on responsibility. *They are installed in it.* Without discussion. Without consent. Without reciprocity.

You may notice:

- You become the emotional regulator
- You carry the relational memory
- You manage conflict fallout
- You absorb stress that is not yours
- You soften the consequences for the other person
- You are expected to remain kind regardless of impact

Over time, the relationship stops responding to you as a person. It responds to you as a function. And functions are not protected. *They are utilised.*

Why Care Becomes Dangerous to the System

Care is dangerous when it remains ***autonomous***—because autonomous care can be withdrawn. It retains choice. It retains timing. It retains the possibility of refusal. And systems organised around control cannot tolerate anything that might one day say *no.*

A nurturing partner who knows their worth is not exploitable. A generous partner with boundaries is not governable. A good-hearted partner who can leave is not controllable. These are not moral judgements; they are structural facts. Care that remains connected to agency cannot be relied upon as infrastructure.

So the system must do something with your care. It cannot leave it free. It cannot allow it to remain voluntary. It must be converted from a gift to a guarantee. It must:

- guilt it
- moralise it
- spiritualise it
- contract it
- normalise its extraction

Each move narrows your freedom while preserving the appearance of virtue. Guilt reframes choice as harm. Moralisation reframes limits as failure. Spiritualisation reframes endurance as goodness. Contracting care turns feeling into obligation. Normalising extraction makes the cost disappear into routine.

This is why goodness is often framed as **duty**. Why love becomes an **obligation**. Why commitment becomes **endurance, what** once flowed freely is now monitored, measured, and enforced.

Your care is no longer something you offer. It is something you **owe**. And once care becomes a liability—once it threatens the system by remaining yours—you will be punished for withholding it, even briefly. Even gently. Even for survival.

Because the system does not fear your anger, it fears your **withdrawal**.

And that is why autonomous care must be disciplined—until it no longer belongs to you at all.

The Cost to the Caregiver

This is where many nurturing partners break down—not because they are weak, but because the system has made their **strength unsustainable**. What once felt like generosity becomes overextension. What once felt like devotion becomes depletion. The body begins to register what the story has been denying: this arrangement cannot continue without damage.

You may feel:

- exhausted without knowing why
- resentful but ashamed of it
- depleted yet responsible
- invisible yet indispensable
- needed but not cherished

Each feeling contradicts the next, and that contradiction is the injury. You are required to give while being denied the conditions that would replenish you. You are relied upon while being disregarded. You are present everywhere except where it matters most—to yourself.

The paradox is brutal:
The more you give, the less you are met.
The more you care, the less you are considered.
The more reliable you become, the more replaceable your humanity feels.

This is not a failure of love. It is a failure of structure. Systems organised around control do not know how to receive care without converting it into fuel. They do not respond to generosity with gratitude; they respond with increased demand. Care is not answered—it is *absorbed.*

Because the system does not love care, it consumes it.

And what is consumed is not just your energy, but your visibility, your voice, your right to rest without consequence. Over time, the caregiver is no longer seen as a person but as a function—something essential yet unnoticed until it falters.

That is the cost that breaks people: not giving too much, but giving into a system that was never designed to give back.

A Necessary Reframe

Care is not meant to be limitless. It is meant to be **reciprocal**. Care exists to move *between* people, not to drain from one into another. When it flows in only one direction, it ceases to be care and becomes a resource.

Care that cannot say *no* is not virtue—it is vulnerability to extraction. It is care stripped of agency, care severed from choice. And care that is punished for setting boundaries is not love. It is **labour**. It is work performed under emotional threat.

And any relationship that requires your goodness to be endlessly available—but never protected—is not honouring your care. It is **feeding on it**. It consumes what it refuses to safeguard.

Closing: When the System Shows Its Hand

Here is the final diagnostic. It is simple, and it is decisive:

When you stop over-giving, does the relationship become curious—or coercive?

If your reduced care is met with concern, repair is possible. Concern signals recognition. It signals a desire to understand what has changed and why.
If it is met with pressure, guilt, rage, or moral framing, clarity arrives. Not emotional clarity—but structural clarity.

Because a system that depends on your goodness will always treat your **autonomy as betrayal**. Not because you are unkind—but because you are no longer extractable. What is being mourned is not connection, but access.

And the moment your care stops being available on demand, the illusion of safety collapses. The calm evaporates. The rules surface. What remains is the truth the system was hiding:

You were valued not for **who you are**—but for **what you were willing to absorb**.

And once you see that, care is no longer your liability.
It becomes your **exit**.

Because care, when reclaimed as choice rather than obligation, stops feeding the system that consumes it—and starts protecting the person who gives it.

✦ Entitlement Without Gratitude ✦

Why access erases appreciation • Why contribution becomes expectation • Why gratitude disappears in hierarchical systems

Gratitude disappears quietly.

Not all at once. Not with cruelty. It does not announce itself as a loss. It does not arrive as hostility. It fades as access becomes assumed and contribution becomes background noise. What was once noticed becomes normal. What was once appreciated becomes expected. What was once thanked becomes required. The transition is subtle enough that many people attribute their sense of its absence to themselves.

This is not forgetfulness. It is structure.
What disappears first is not love. It is recognition.

Gratitude is a signal. It marks recognition. It states: "*I still know you are a person.*" It states: "*I still remember this is yours to give.*" It acknowledges that care, effort, presence, and labour arise from choice rather than obligation. Gratitude keeps a relationship alive by keeping the contribution visible.

When gratitude disappears, something structural has replaced something relational. The relationship has ceased to regard you as a subject and has begun to regard you as a function. Your giving has moved from being *received* to being *counted on.* And what is counted on is no longer acknowledged—it is scheduled.

In control-based systems, gratitude is unsustainable because it implies **dependence**, which threatens hierarchy. To thank you would be to admit need. To recognise your contribution would be to acknowledge vulnerability. Expressing appreciation would involve recognising that the system does not function without you.

So gratitude must erode. Slowly. Quietly. Without announcement.

*Because once your care is no longer thanked, it can be **assumed**.*
*And once it is assumed, it can be **extracted**.*
And once it is extracted, it no longer belongs to you.

That is the final shift to notice: the disappearance of gratitude is not emotional neglect—it is **structural conversion**. It is the moment your humanity is no longer met but only *used.*

And when gratitude is gone, what has replaced love is not indifference.
It is entitlement.

Why Access Erases Appreciation

Access changes perception. Not morally, but structurally. Not because people become cruel, but because familiarity alters what the nervous system registers as remarkable.

When someone has to ask, they notice. When someone has to earn, they appreciate. When someone has to risk losing, they stay aware. Effort sharpens perception. Uncertainty keeps attention alive.

But when access becomes **guaranteed**—when your time, care, labour, body, loyalty, and availability are assumed—attention dulls. What was once consciously received becomes unconsciously relied upon.

You are no longer experienced as a gift. You are experienced as part of the environment. Built-in things are rarely thanked. *Electricity is not praised until it goes out.* The more essential something becomes, the more invisible it is treated.

This is why appreciation often peaks early and declines sharply once access is secured. Not because your value diminished—but because it was stabilised into the background.

At first:
"I can't believe how much you do."
"I've never had anyone like you."
"I'm so grateful for you."

Later:
silence,
impatience,
irritation when you hesitate,
surprise when you say no.

When you give, it is invisible. When you hesitate, it is offensive. The presence of expectation replaces the absence of gratitude.

Not because your contribution decreased—but because **access erased awareness.**

Gratitude requires ***recognition****. Recognition requires* ***separateness****.* Hierarchy dissolves both. Hierarchy depends on assumed access and uninterrupted flow. Gratitude equalises. It acknowledges dependence. And equalisation threatens advantage.

So appreciation fades—not accidentally, but predictably. Because once your presence is treated as infrastructure, thanking you would require acknowledging that the system does not function without you.

And that is what control cannot afford to say.

Why Contribution Becomes Expectation

Contribution is meant to circulate. It is meant to move, to respond, to flow between people in rhythm with circumstance and care. In its healthy form, the contribution remains **visible** because it remains **voluntary.**

In healthy relationships, effort is reciprocal. Care is mirrored. Support is responsive. No one's giving becomes invisible because no one's giving is taken for granted. Contribution remains relational: it responds to need, not entitlement; to context, not command.

However, in hierarchical systems, contributions are **reclassified**. Not suddenly, not aggressively, but quietly—through repetition and assumption.

It ceases to be something you offer and becomes something you **are for**.

Your actions are no longer read as choices. They are read as functions.

The shift is subtle but decisive:
what you do once becomes what you "always" do;
what you do generously becomes what you "handle";
what you do voluntarily becomes what you're "good at";
what you do out of love becomes your "role".

Each step sounds benign. Each step feels almost complementary. But together they convert generosity into identity. And once something becomes your role, gratitude feels unnecessary. ***Roles are not thanked; they are relied upon.***

Praise becomes ***precedent****.*
Precedent becomes ***policy****.*
And once policy is in place, deviation is treated not as a choice, but as a failure.
Why thank a system for functioning?

Expectation replaces appreciation because expectation preserves **hierarchy**. Expectation keeps contribution predictable, uninterrupted, and unequal. Gratitude would acknowledge dependence—acknowledge that the system benefits from you, relies on you, and would falter without you.

And that acknowledgement is dangerous.

Because once dependence is admitted, power must be renegotiated.
And hierarchy does not survive renegotiation.

Why Gratitude Disappears in Hierarchical Systems

Gratitude is incompatible with dominance. Not emotionally, but structurally. Gratitude alters the balance of power simply by existing.

To be grateful is to admit you received something you could not produce alone. It acknowledges dependence. It recognises contribution as **voluntary rather than owed**. It says: *this came from you, and you did not have to give it.* That admission levels the field. It restores agency to the giver.

Hierarchy cannot afford that.

In a hierarchical system, roles must remain fixed and flows predictable. Gratitude disrupts both. It introduces mutual recognition where asymmetry is required. So it quietly erodes.

In a hierarchical system:

- One person's giving is framed as a duty
- The other's receiving is framed as entitlement
- Imbalance is normalised
- Contribution flows upward
- Appreciation does not flow back down

These are not personal failures. They are design features. Gratitude would expose the system's dependence on the very person it seeks to subordinate. It would reveal that what is framed as an obligation is, in fact, a gift.

This is why gratitude often disappears precisely when your contribution

increases. The more essential you become, the more dangerous it is to acknowledge you.

You are thanked when you are optional.
You are unthanked when you are essential.

Once you are essential, gratitude would acknowledge the **leverage** you are not meant to have. It would imply that you could withdraw. That you could choose differently. That the system does not function without you.

And hierarchy cannot survive that truth being spoken aloud.

The Emotional Shift People Feel but Can't Name

This is often the stage where people say, *"I don't feel appreciated anymore."* They struggle to articulate what has changed, because nothing obvious has happened. There may be no single incident, no dramatic rupture, no precise moment of betrayal. Just a quiet internal recognition that something fundamental has shifted.

But what they are sensing is more precise than that. It is not simply the absence of praise. It is not just emotional neglect. It is a change in *how they are being perceived.*

They feel entitled to.

Not noticed. Not met. Not encountered. ***Used.***

They feel like:

- Their effort no longer registers
- Their labour is assumed
- Their presence is consumed
- Their withdrawal would cause outrage, not concern
- Their exhaustion is irrelevant
- Their limits are treated as an inconvenience.

Each of these sensations points to the same underlying transformation. Contribution has ceased to be recognised as choice. Care has ceased to be received as a gift. The relationship has stopped responding to *who they are* and started relying on *what they provide.*

They are not being seen as a person contributing. They are treated as a **resource for maintaining the system**. And resources are not thanked.

They are managed.

This is the emotional shift people struggle to name—not a lack of love, but a loss of personhood. The moment you realise that your presence is valued only for its function is the moment appreciation quietly disappears, because the system no longer sees you as someone who gives.

It sees you as something that keeps it running.

Why Asking for Gratitude Triggers Resistance

When gratitude has disappeared, asking for it often backfires. Not because the request is unreasonable, but because it threatens the **structure** that has quietly replaced the relationship.

Because the moment gratitude must be named, the system is forced to acknowledge something it has been working to erase: that what you give is *optional*, not owed.

"Can you acknowledge what I do?"
"I feel unappreciated."
"I need to feel valued."

These are not demands for praise. They are requests for recognition. They are attempts to restore relational reality.

In mutual systems, these requests invite reflection. They slow the interaction down. They open a space to notice impact, imbalance, and repair. They are received as information.

In hierarchical systems, they provoke defensiveness, dismissal, or moral framing:

"You shouldn't need thanks."
"That's just part of being a partner."
"You're keeping score."
"You're too sensitive."
"I never asked you to do that."

Each response performs the same function: it denies your agency while preserving access to your labour. It reframes your giving as automatic. It recasts your exhaustion as inappropriate. It converts your request into a character flaw.

The subtext is clear:

Your contribution does not entitle you to recognition.
Your giving does not entitle you to a voice.
Your exhaustion does not entitle you to relief.

Because relief would require acknowledging **cost, and** cost would require recognising **your choice**. And choice would expose the lie on which the system depends: that your care is simply how things are, not something you are actively doing.

Once gratitude is granted, entitlement is exposed. Gratitude would require admitting **dependence**. Dependence would require **humility**. And humility would collapse the hierarchy.

So gratitude must be resisted—not because it is excessive, but because it is **structurally dangerous**.

Because once someone thanks you sincerely, they admit they need you. And once need is admitted, power can no longer pretend it stands alone.

The Final Inversion

Here is the cruellest inversion in these systems. Not a misunderstanding. Not a miscommunication. An inversion that operates with mechanical precision once hierarchy is installed:

The more you give, the less gratitude you receive.
The less gratitude you receive, the more you are told to give "freely".
The more you give "freely", the less free you become.

Each step is framed as a virtue. Each step sounds moral. Each step is defended as maturity. But together they form a closed loop that drains agency while praising sacrifice.

And eventually, something clicks. Not dramatically. Quietly. With the clarity that arrives when a pattern can no longer be denied.

You realise that you are not appreciated because appreciation implies **choice**. And choice would imply **power**. It would acknowledge that you could stop. That you could withdraw. That what you give is not guaranteed.

So gratitude is removed—not accidentally, not gradually, not out of forgetfulness—but **structurally and removed** because it interferes with extraction. Removed because it destabilises entitlement. Removed because it would remind you that your giving is yours.

And that is the final truth this inversion reveals:
the system does not want your care to feel chosen.
It wants it to feel *inevitable*.

Because inevitability keeps you giving.
And gratitude might remind you that you don't have to.

A Clean Diagnostic

Ask yourself this—not rhetorically, not abstractly, but as a grounded assessment of how the relationship actually *responds* to you:

Does my contribution make the other person more grateful—or more entitled?

This question cuts through explanation, intention, and hope. It does not ask what they say. It asks what your giving *produces*.

In healthy love, contribution produces **softness**. It creates tenderness, humility, and increased care. It deepens attunement. It makes the other person more aware of your humanity, not less. Your giving is met, noticed, and held with care because it is recognised as *yours*.

In control-based systems, contribution produces **appetite**. It does not satisfy; it stimulates demand. The more you give, the more the system recalibrates around what else it can take. Your effort is not received as a gift, but logged as capacity.

If giving more makes the system **lean back** rather than lean in—if it relaxes into entitlement instead of rising into reciprocity—you are not being partnered. You are not being met. You are not being held with care.

You are being consumed.

And once you see that clearly, the question is no longer whether you should give more.

The question becomes whether you are willing to keep feeding something that grows stronger by **taking you in.**

The Quiet End of the Illusion

Gratitude is often the last thing to go. Not because it matters least—but because it is the final signal of recognition, the last trace of relational seeing before structure fully replaces connection.

People will tolerate imbalance.
They will tolerate exhaustion.
They will tolerate unfairness.
They will tolerate silence.
They will explain it. Minimise it. Normalise it. Carry it longer than they should.

However, the absence of gratitude has a **specific** physiological effect. It bypasses rationalisation. It enters the nervous system directly.

It tells you: *I am not seen.*
I am not chosen.
I am not valued for my humanity.
I am valued for my output.

This is not emotional neglect. It is a **functional reassignment**.

Infrastructure is maintained, not cherished. Infrastructure is relied upon, not thanked. And when infrastructure begins to fail, it is not comforted; it is **replaced**.

And once that truth lands, something irreversible happens. Not explosively. Quietly. With a calm that feels unfamiliar.

You stop giving with your heart.
You start conserving.
You start noticing.
You start preparing to leave.

Not because you are cold. Not because you are cruel. But because your body understands something your hope was trying to outrun.

Because love without gratitude is not love.

It is **entitlement** that no longer bothers to say thank you.

And the moment you stop mistaking entitlement for normalcy, the system loses what it depended on most: **your willingness to give without being honoured**.

That is not bitterness.
That is clarity.

Illusion does not end with drama. It ends with **clarity**. Not with confrontation, not with collapse, not with spectacle—but with seeing the moment when confusion can no longer be sustained.

Up to this point, the system has survived by misnaming itself: calling **control** care, calling **certainty** safety, calling **extraction** love. It has relied on confusion, on goodwill, on your willingness to explain, endure, and give meaning where none was offered. It has depended on your capacity to translate harm into misunderstanding and imbalance into accident.

But illusion has a fatal weakness: **it cannot survive being seen**.

Once the patterns are named, the system loses its disguise. Once motives are clear, leverage dissolves. Once reality is spoken plainly, the structure has nothing left to negotiate with. There is no longer ambiguity to exploit, no misunderstanding to correct, no hope to stretch thinner.

This is where control does not escalate—it **collapses**.

Not because you fight harder, but because you stop participating. Not because you win, but because you withdraw the fuel that kept the system alive: confusion, justification, self-doubt, and endless explanation.

Part IV begins at the moment the system realises you are no longer confused, no longer bargaining, no longer asking to be met halfway. You are simply standing in what you see, and refusing to move.

And that is the moment everything changes.
Because control can survive **anger, it** cannot survive **clarity**.

What follows is not reconciliation.
It is the end of the system's power.

This is the moment of choice.

Not whether you will be understood, but whether you will continue to give your life to something that requires you *not* to understand in order to exist.

IV

✦ THE MOMENT OF CHOICE ✦

Why clarity ends the system

This is the point where the system stops working.
Not because you fight it—but because you see it.
Control survives confusion, negotiation, and even anger.
It does not survive clarity. Once patterns are named, leverage dissolves.

Once reality is spoken plainly, the structure loses its grip.
What follows is not escalation or repair.
It is collapse.
This section begins where explanation ends and refusal becomes possible.

✦ A Note on Clarity, Safety, and Exposure ✦

Clarity does not require confrontation.
Naming does not require exposure.
And safety, in some contexts, requires **invisibility**.

These distinctions matter because not all systems respond to being seen in the same way. Some systems escalate when they are seen. Some retaliate when patterns are named publicly.
Some protect themselves through **denial**, **character attack**, or **narrative reversal** when their structure is threatened. Visibility, in these environments, is not neutral. It carries risk.

This section explains **why systems collapse when clarity appears**—not how, when, or whether you should reveal what you see. It is not a call to disclosure. It is not a demand for testimony. It is an explanation of the mechanism, not a prescription for action. Silence, distance, and withdrawal are not failures of courage here.
They are often **intelligent responses** to environments that punish perception.
They are strategic acts of self-preservation, not evidence of fear.

This work is not asking you to become visible before you are protected, or honest before it is safe. It is not asking you to perform your clarity

for anyone else's understanding.
It is asking you to become **clear**—internally, quietly, decisively—and to let that clarity guide your choices without requiring performance.

Because clarity does not need an audience.
And safety does not require explanation.

✦ Why Exposure Shuts Systems Down ✦

Why naming patterns are destabilising • Why clarity removes leverage • Why explanation is unnecessary

E**xposure is not confrontation.** Exposure is contact with reality. It is the moment illusion loses insulation. It is what occurs when perception stops being negotiated and begins to be trusted.

Control-based systems do not collapse because you become louder. They collapse because you become **accurate**—because accuracy removes the fog they need to operate. Fog blurs responsibility. Fog softens the consequence. Fog keeps power unlocatable. Once something is named, it can no longer pretend to be harmless, accidental, or misunderstood.

This is why so many controlling dynamics are sustained by **atmosphere rather than events**, **tone rather than truth**, **ambiguity rather than agreement**. The system does not need you to believe it is good. It only requires you to doubt yourself enough to keep cooperating. Doubt keeps you explaining. Doubt keeps you adjusting. Doubt keeps you available.

Exposure ends that. Not with accusation. Not with performance. Not with a spectacle.

With a **clean sentence**.

A sentence that does not argue.
A sentence that does not justify.
A sentence that simply *names what is happening*.

And once reality is spoken cleanly—even if only to yourself—the system loses its most powerful resource: your confusion.

Because control can survive anger.
It can survive resistance.
It can even survive distance.

But it cannot survive accuracy.

Accuracy does not fight the system.
It renders it obsolete.

Why Naming Patterns Is Destabilising

A pattern is not a complaint.
A pattern is a structure.

This distinction matters. Complaints can be soothed, reframed, or apologised away. Structures cannot. Structures explain outcomes regardless of intention. They reveal design.

When you name a pattern, you are no longer discussing a moment. You are describing an **architecture**: what happens repeatedly, predictably, regardless of intentions and apologies. You are no longer responding to behaviour; you are mapping how behaviour is organised.

This is destabilising because control relies on **fragmentation and ambiguity**. It survives when events remain disconnected—when each incident can be treated as isolated, context-free, and deniable:

It was a bad day.
You took it the wrong way.
That's not what I meant.
Why are you making this a thing?

Each sentence breaks continuity. Each one severs cause from pattern. Each one invites you back into confusion.

Pattern-naming refuses isolation. It links the moments into a **design**. It shows recurrence. It reveals predictability. And once a design is seen, the system loses its favourite defence: **plausible innocence**. There is no longer room to pretend each instance was accidental, unrelated, or misunderstood.

This is why exposure often triggers an immediate shift—not because the words were harsh, but because they were **organising**. Organisation removes deniability. It replaces emotional debate with structural clarity.

You are no longer negotiating feelings.
You are describing **mechanics**.

You are not asking, *Can we talk about it?*
You are saying, *This is what keeps happening.*

That sentence is a threat to any system built on your staying confused.

Because confusion keeps you responsive, confusion keeps you hopeful. Confusion keeps you trying.

Clarity does none of those things.

And that is why naming patterns destabilise control—not by accusation, but by **ending fragmentation**. Once the fragments are assembled, the system is exposed for what it is.

Not a misunderstanding.
A design.

Why Clarity Removes Leverage

Leverage needs darkness. Not literal darkness—**interpretive darkness**. The half-light in which meaning remains unstable and outcomes remain negotiable. The space where you keep explaining, adjusting, waiting, and second-guessing. The space where your decency is used as a delay. Where time stretches, accountability blurs, and responsibility never quite lands.

Clarity ends that space.

Because leverage is not created only through power, it is created through your willingness to keep offering access while you are uncertain. Through your continued presence, even as you hope it will make sense. Through your patience while you are still trying to be fair.

When you become clear, you stop offering the currency control runs on:

- extra chances
- benefit of the doubt as a lifestyle
- endless emotional labour
- rehearsed conversations that go nowhere
- "Maybe I'm overreacting"
- "I don't want to be unfair"
- "Let me say it better"

Each of these once felt like integrity. Each of them once felt like care. But together they form the **loop** that sustains the system. They keep you available without resolution. They keep the system supplied without cost.

Clarity eliminates the back-and-forth in which the system regains ground. It removes the delay. It removes the bargaining posture. You stop feeding the loop. You stop negotiating for fundamental reciprocity. You stop trying to make your reality acceptable to someone who benefits from it remaining blurred.

And that is why clarity feels like an **earthquake** to them. Not because you are doing something aggressive, but because something essential has disappeared.

Because what they have been managing is not you.
It is your **uncertainty**.

Once uncertainty is gone, leverage collapses. There is nothing left to press on, nothing left to stall with, nothing left to extract through confusion. The system does not lose control because you confront it.

It loses control because there is nothing left for it to work with.

Clarity is not resistance.
Clarity is **withdrawal from the fog**.

And systems built on fog cannot function in daylight.

Why Explanation Is Unnecessary

Explanation is often a form of **permission-seeking**. It carries a quiet hope: that if you present your case gently enough, clearly enough, kindly enough, the other person will finally become reasonable—that if you can prove your pain in the correct language, it will be honoured. It assumes misunderstanding is the obstacle and that clarity will produce care.

But systems do not fail because they lack understanding. They fail because understanding would require **surrender**—of advantage, of control, of position.

A controlling structure requires no additional information. It requires you to keep believing that information will change it. As long as you believe this, you stay engaged. You keep explaining. You stay available.

This is why explanation becomes a **trap**:

You explain → they reinterpret.
You clarify → they debate.
You provide examples → they minimise.
You name impact → they critique tone.
You ask for change → they promise vaguely.

You relax → the pattern returns.

Nothing here is accidental. Nothing here is confused. Each move preserves the system while exhausting you. The loop is not a failure of communication—it is the communication.

The system is not confused.
It is **calibrated**.

So, explanation is not the tool that ends it.
Exposure is.

Exposure does not argue.
It **names**.

What Exposure Actually Looks Like

Exposure is often quiet. It does not perform certainty; it embodies it. It can be as small as:

- "I've noticed the pattern: when I ask for fairness, you escalate."
- "I'm not confused. I'm clear."
- "This isn't a misunderstanding. It's a structure."
- "I won't keep discussing what you keep repeating."
- "Your reactions are the answer."

These sentences do not persuade. They do not invite debate. They remove oxygen from the system by withdrawing confusion. They end the performance of the uncertainty on which the structure depended.

Exposure is not about convincing them. It is about **removing your**

participation from a system that required your confusion to function.

When you do that, the dynamic enters its most revealing phase: the moment the mechanism tries to survive **without disguise**.

Because once charm fails, and silence fails, and negotiation fails—there is only one tool left:

enforcement.

And enforcement can no longer pretend to be love.

The Moment the System Realises You Can See

There is a particular kind of shift that happens when a controlling system detects **clarity**. It is not dramatic. It is not loud. It is precise. Something in the dynamic reorients when something essential is lost.

The conversation stops being **relational**.
It becomes **positional**.

You are no longer being engaged as a person whose experience matters. You are being assessed as a variable that has changed. The system is no longer trying to connect. It is trying to **contain**.

You will often perceive it as *temperature* rather than volume. The shift does not need raised voices to be unmistakable:

- sudden coldness
- contempt that arrives too quickly
- rigid certainty

- refusal to engage with the actual point
- subtle punishment for having sight

Each signal communicates the same message: *you have crossed from participant to threat.* Not because you demanded too much—but because you stopped misreading what was happening.

This is not because you said it wrong.
It is because you said it in a way that leaves **no room for denial**.

Exposure is destabilising because it returns you to **yourself**. It restores internal authority. It ends the habit of outsourcing meaning to the other person's reactions. And that is what control cannot tolerate: **a person who no longer negotiates their own perception**.

Once you trust what you see, the system loses its leverage.
Once you stop doubting your reality, there is nothing left to manage.

That is the moment the system realises you can see.

Closing

Exposure shuts systems down because control depends on your cooperation with **confusion**. It requires you to keep misreading what is happening, to keep translating harm into misunderstanding, to keep granting time and access while certainty is delayed. Naming patterns destabilise because they turn incidents into **architecture**—because once behaviour is seen as design, it can no longer hide behind apology or intent. Clarity removes leverage by ending the currency of **uncertainty**. Explanation is unnecessary because the system was never missing information—only your willingness to keep hoping.

This is the moment the book has been moving towards.

Not the moment you become harsher.
The moment you become exact.

Exactness is not cruelty. It is precision. It is the refusal to dilute what you see in order to preserve comfort. It is the decision to stop cushioning reality so the system can continue to function.

Because once you can name what is happening, you stop asking whether you're allowed to leave. You stop waiting for permission. You stop waiting for proof. You stop waiting for the system to agree with your reality. You stop bargaining for validation from the very structure that required your doubt.

And the system, for the first time, has to face something it cannot manage:

A person who can see.

Clarity does not obligate action. Seeing a pattern does not require you to respond, confront, explain, or reveal what you know. There is no moral demand to announce your understanding. Sometimes the most accurate move is **no move at all**—quiet disengagement while your life reorganises around what is now clear.

Because clarity is not a performance.
It is an internal shift.

And once that shift occurs, the system's power is already over—whether it realises it yet or not.

✦ Why Naming Beats Anger ✦

Why anger feeds the system • Why precision collapses it • Why calm refusal is more threatening

Precision is dangerous because it produces **no footage**. There is nothing to replay, nothing to misquote, nothing to sensationalise. It leaves no spectacle behind. It does not give the system material to work with.

Anger feels like power. It feels active. It feels justified. It feels like movement. But to a control-based system, it is **nourishment**—not because your anger is wrong, not because it is unjustified, but because it is **usable**. Anger can be redirected. It can be framed. It can be provoked, harvested, and then displayed as evidence against you.

Anger produces **noise**.
Noise produces **distortion**.
Distortion restores **advantage**.

Once distortion enters, clarity is lost. Once clarity is lost, the system regains room to manoeuvre. Tone becomes the focus. Delivery becomes the argument. Your reaction becomes the story. And the original reality disappears behind the performance of conflict.

This is why so many people are provoked into anger and then punished for it—not accidentally, not unfairly, but **structurally**. The provocation is not a mistake. It is a strategy. Anger supplies the system with what it needs: distraction, misdirection, and moral cover.

Some systems do not fear being challenged.
They fear being **seen**.

And when they feel seen, they do not reflect. They do not soften. They do not repair.

They become **tactical**.

They look for footage.
They look for tone.
They look for something they can point to and say, *See? This is the problem.*

Precision denies them that. Precision gives them nothing to work with. No spectacle. No distortion. No leverage.

That is why precision is quieter—and more dangerous—than anger.

Because anger keeps you in the arena.
Precision ends the game.

Why Anger Feeds the System

Anger externalises your energy. It raises volume, accelerates pace, shortens nuance, and makes you reactive instead of exact. What was once precise becomes diffuse. What was once grounded becomes kinetic.

Anger moves you outward, away from the centre of your perception and into the terrain of response.

And reaction is the system's **favourite terrain**.

When you are angry, three things happen that benefit control. These are not accidental side-effects; they are structural advantages.

Your message becomes **editable**.
Tone replaces content. Your accuracy is dismissed as emotion; your clarity is reframed as instability. What you say becomes secondary to *how* you said it.

Your reaction becomes **the story**.
The focus shifts from what happened to how you responded. The original issue recedes. Your behaviour becomes the evidence.

Material is **created**.
Anger provides moments that can be replayed, excerpted, exaggerated, or circulated—not to understand you, but to reframe you.

A control-based system will often provoke you privately, document you selectively, and remain calm while you carry the heat. It stays still while you move. It records while you react. It watches while you burn.

Your worst moment becomes evidence.
Their consistent pattern disappears.

This is why anger so often triggers character attacks, concern-trolling ("I'm worried about you"), reputational smearing, sudden narratives about your "issues", and selective memory of your weakest moment.

The system need not address what it has done. It only needs something else to point at.

Not because you lost control.
Because the system **gained leverage**.

Control does not need you to be silent.
It requires you to be **disprovable**.

Anger keeps you in the field of play.

Why Precision Collapses It

Precision does the opposite of anger. It removes excess. It slows the moment. It narrows the field. Precision does not explain your feelings. It names the **mechanism**. It does not dramatise. It delineates.

Examples of precision are not speeches. They are sentences:

"When I set a boundary, you withdraw."
"Fairness leads to escalation here."
"This dynamic depends on me doubting myself."
"I'm not engaging with this pattern anymore."

Precision is threatening because it leaves **no opening**. There is nothing to argue with. Nothing to correct. Nothing to misquote without noticeable distortion. No emotional surplus to exploit. No reaction to redirect.

You are not making a case.
You are stating a **recognition**.

And, recognition collapses control by removing **ambiguity**—the very thing the system needs to function. Ambiguity creates motion. Ambiguity creates hope. Ambiguity keeps you engaged.

Where anger expands the interaction, **precision ends it**.

Not with force.
Not with a spectacle.
But with exactness so clean, the system has nowhere left to stand.

Why Calm Refusal Is More Threatening

Calm refusal is the most destabilising move available. Not because it is dramatic, not because it asserts dominance, but because it withdraws something the system assumed was guaranteed.

Not refusal as protest.
Refusal as **withdrawal of participation**.

When you refuse calmly, you are not asking to be understood, not trying to be validated, not inviting negotiation, and not performing pain. You are not presenting an argument or staging resistance. You are not making yourself legible for assessment.

You are simply **no longer available**.

This is terrifying to a system organised around access.

- Access to your time.
- Access to your energy.
- Access to your responsiveness.

- Access to your willingness to keep engaging.

Because anger says, "*I am still engaged.*"
Calm refusal states: "*I have exited the structure.*"

Calm refusal cannot be reframed as hysteria. It cannot be baited into escalation. It does not provide footage. It does not create scenes. There is no spike of emotion to capture, no excess to distort, no reaction to provoke.

It leaves nothing that can be replayed, edited, or turned into a story about you.

It leaves the system with **nothing to work with**.

This is why calm refusal is often met with sudden urgency, artificial calm, moral pressure, last-minute concessions, or abrupt disappearance. The system scrambles—not to reconnect, but to regain traction.

Not because you are wrong.
Because the system has **lost traction**.

The Strategic Truth Most People Miss

You do not need to be louder to be effective.
You need to be **less usable**.

Anger makes you usable.
Explanation makes you usable.
Defence makes you usable.

Each one supplies energy, material, and engagement. Each one keeps you in the field of play.

Naming does not.

Naming turns a lived experience into a **visible structure**—and then steps away. It does not stay to argue. It does not stay to persuade. It does not stay to soften what has been seen.

This is why people who name clearly are often called *cold*, *detached*, *cruel*, *unloving*, or *unreasonable.*

These are not descriptions.

They are **symptoms** of a system that no longer has access to your energy.

What This Chapter Is Actually Teaching

This chapter is not telling you to suppress anger.

Anger is information. It tells you a boundary has been crossed, dignity has been violated, and reality is being challenged. It is a signal, not a flaw.

But anger is not a **strategy**.

Strategy is choosing the move that costs the system the most and costs you the least. Strategy is not about winning expression; it is about ending exposure.

And that move is

- **clarity without heat**.
- **Precision without performance**.
- **Refusal without explanation**.

The Quiet Shift That Changes Everything

There is a moment—often unnoticed—when a person stops trying to be believed and starts acting on what they already know. It does not arrive with confrontation. It does not announce itself as courage. It arises from internal alignment, when perception no longer needs confirmation and truth no longer requires permission.

Their voice lowers.
Their sentences are shortened.
Their availability ends.

What disappears is not feeling, but performance. What ends is not care, but negotiation with denial.

They do not win the argument. They end the **dynamic, not** by overpowering it, but by stepping out of the role that sustained it.

That is why naming beats anger. Anger keeps the system central. Naming recentres **you**. It moves attention away from reaction and back to authorship. It restores the axis of choice.

Not because anger is weak—but because **clarity is final**. Anger can be absorbed, redirected, or reframed. Clarity cannot. It does not escalate. It concludes.

And systems built on leverage cannot survive finality. They require motion, doubt, engagement, and response. They cannot function when there is nothing left to negotiate.

In the next chapter, we move into the act that follows naming naturally—not escalation, not defence, not disappearance yet—but **refusal**. Not refusal as rebellion, but refusal as authorship.

The moment agency returns to the person who was never meant to keep it.

✦ The Power of Refusal ✦

Why refusal reclaims agency • Why it provokes retreat, not pursuit • Why dignity is non-negotiable

Refusal is not anger with better manners.

It is not a protest. It is not an explanation. It does not argue its case or justify its timing. It does not seek to be understood or validated.

Refusal is the moment you **stop participating**.

Refusal is the **withdrawal of access**.
Access to your attention.
Access to your emotional labour.
Access to your reflex to engage, soothe, clarify, and repair. Access to the part of you that kept responding long after clarity arrived.

Nothing dramatic happens. No verdict is delivered. No victory speech is required. There is no confrontation to memorialise, no exchange to replay. The absence of spectacle is the point.

You simply withdraw the one resource the system cannot function without: **your cooperation**.

That is why refusal is **final**.

Why Refusal Reclaims Agency

Agency is not reclaimed by winning arguments. It is reclaimed by ending the **premise**. Control depends on response—on correction, engagement, and your continued orientation toward repair while the structure remains unchanged. It survives on your willingness to keep addressing symptoms rather than withdrawing from the design. Refusal breaks that orientation.

When you refuse, three things happen at once:

- You stop negotiating your **perception**.
- You stop offering your **nervous system** as leverage.
- You stop translating your **reality** into something acceptable.

Each shift removes a point of access that the system relied on. Each one restores authorship where compliance once lived.

Refusal does not ask to be understood. It assumes understanding is complete enough to leave. This is the quiet shift from reacting *inside* the system to standing *outside* it—from "What can I say?" to "I'm done saying." From "How do I fix this?" to "This does not get access."

Agency returns not because you asserted harder, but because you **withdrew consent**. Not loudly. Not theatrically. Decisively.

You are no longer negotiating reality.
You are **choosing** it.

And once choice replaces negotiation, the system has nothing left to work with.

Why Refusal Provokes Retreat, Not Pursuit

Control escalates when it senses **confusion**. It retreats when it senses **finality**. Escalation feeds on uncertainty; retreat follows recognition that uncertainty is gone. Pursuit requires hope—hope that you can be moved, softened, provoked, guilted, or drawn back into dialogue. Hope that something in you is still responsive, still pliable, still available.

Refusal removes that hope.

Refusal offers no hooks:

- No anger to frame
- No explanation to dismantle
- No emotion to manage
- No debate to reopen

What remains is a **closed door** with no handle on its side. There is no entry point, no leverage point, no emotional grip left to apply pressure to. The absence of access is unmistakable.

This is why, after refusal, you often see a rapid sequence: sudden politeness, artificial calm, last-minute concessions, moral pressure, or abrupt disappearance. These are not signs of resolution. They are **exit behaviours**—the system tests whether access can be restored, then withdraws when it cannot.

Control does not chase what it cannot govern. Control is not love. **It is**

efficiency.

Why Dignity Is Non-Negotiable

Dignity is not a feeling. It is a ***line****.* It is the line you do not cross, and the line you do not allow others to cross on your behalf. It is the decision—quiet, firm, and non-negotiable—that your humanity is not a bargaining chip, your safety not a price, your clarity not a provocation. It is not mood-dependent. It is not situational. It does not fluctuate with approval.

Dignity does not ask permission to exist.

This is why refusal feels *cold* to those who relied on your warmth; why it feels *cruel* to those who depended on your patience; why it is framed as abandonment by those who treated access as entitlement. When someone has organised their comfort around your availability, your withdrawal registers not as a boundary but as a threat.

But dignity does not require approval.
It requires consistency.

Refusal is dignity enacted—**calm**, **exact**, and unresponsive to pressure. It does not justify itself. It does not apologise for existing. It does not negotiate with systems that require your diminishment. It does not soften to preserve connection at the cost of self-respect.

Once dignity becomes non-negotiable, the relationship changes **categories**. It is no longer relational. It is **administrative**. Administrative structures cannot survive without compliance.

When compliance ends, the structure does too.

What Refusal Looks Like in Practice

Refusal is brief. It is boring. It does not escalate. It does not argue its case or attempt to manage the other person's reaction. It is intentionally uninteresting to a system that feeds on drama, negotiation, and emotional movement.

"I won't participate in this."
"That doesn't work for me."
"I'm done with this conversation."
"My decision stands."

These sentences are not explanations. They are closures. They do not invite response; they end access. Each one draws a boundary that does not require agreement to be real.

No postscript.
No softening.
No second round.

Refusal does not linger to soothe discomfort or repair the other person's feelings about your boundary. It does not stay to witness the reaction. It leaves the moment intact and exits.

Refusal is not silence born of fear.
It is silence born of **completion**.

Completion means the internal work has already been done. The decision has already been made. There is nothing left to process aloud, nothing left to clarify, nothing left to negotiate.

The conversation ends because **the system no longer has access**, not because you have run out of words.

And that is what makes refusal so powerful: it is not reactive. It is resolved.

The Irreversible Shift

There is a moment—often understated—when the system realises something essential has changed: **you are no longer persuadable**. The shift is subtle, almost invisible from the outside, but internally it is absolute. What disappears is not emotion, but access. What ends is not discussion, but leverage.

At that point, the dynamic does not evolve. It **ends**—either visibly or quietly. Not because you won, not because the other person conceded, but because the terms of engagement no longer exist. There is nothing left to negotiate, no uncertainty left to exploit, no hope left that you can be moved back into participation.

This is the power of **refusal**. It does not fix the system. It does not reform it. It does not seek justice from it. It renders it **irrelevant**.

And once relevance is gone, control has nothing left to do.

Not rage.
Not explanation.
Not repair.

Only retreat—or disappearance.

Which is where we go next.

✦ When They Don't Retaliate – They Disappear ✦

Why silence follows exposure · Why control collapses inward · Why some losses are never spoken of again

Sometimes there is no retaliation.
No rage.
No smear campaign.
No final fight.

There is just... absence. Not the absence of confusion, not the absence of feeling, but the sudden lack of engagement itself. Because when exposure lands cleanly—when the pattern is named, the leverage is gone, the access is refused—the system doesn't always strike back.

This is the moment many people misread. They expect noise. They brace for punishment. They wait for escalation, confrontation, or revenge. But what comes instead is quieter—and far more telling.

Sometimes it does something colder.

It disappears.

Not as grief. As a strategy.

This disappearance is not a withdrawal born of reflection or remorse. It is not the space taken to process. It is not respect for boundaries. It is a calculated withdrawal from a field in which control is no longer viable. A system that cannot operate in clarity does not adapt to it. It exits it.

And that absence is not peace.
It is collapse.

Collapse does not always announce itself as destruction. Sometimes it looks like quiet. Sometimes it looks like indifference. Sometimes it looks like someone is suddenly no longer present, no longer reactive, no longer invested. But this is not healing distance. It is a structural failure. It is the moment the system realises it cannot proceed without disguise—and chooses disappearance over exposure.

Because when a system is seen clearly, it has only two options: transform or retreat. And systems organised around control do not transform. They disengage.

What vanishes is not the relationship. What vanishes is the mechanism that depended on your confusion to survive.

And once that mechanism is gone, what remains is not resolution, not reconciliation, not closure—but truth, standing quietly where the noise used to be.

That silence is not empty.

It is diagnostic.

Why Silence Follows Exposure

Silence is not always confusion. Sometimes it is calculation. Exposure removes the system's favourite terrain: ambiguity. It collapses plausible deniability. It makes every future move legible. So the system goes quiet—not because it has nothing to say, but because speaking now costs too much.

If it argues, it confirms the structure.
If it explains, it admits the structure.
If it apologises, it lowers itself into mutuality.
If it attacks, it reveals itself.

So the system takes the cleanest option left: *withdrawal without explanation.*

Silence is the only move that preserves the illusion. This is why the silence after exposure feels different from the silence before. Before, silence was used to recalibrate *you*. After, *silence is used to protect them.* It is the system withdrawing its hand because it has been observed.

Why Control Collapses Inward

Control depends on outward motion: your attention, your engagement, your questions, your proving, your emotional labour. When you refuse participation, the system loses its external engine. And without that engine, control has nowhere to go.

It cannot build a new reality inside your nervous system. It cannot keep you in the loop. It cannot keep you half-sure and fully invested. So it collapses inward. **Disappearance is economy.**

This is what people misread as “maturity” or “acceptance”. It isn’t. It is conservation.

A control-based structure will often withdraw the moment it realises:

- You are no longer persuadable
- You are no longer baitable
- You are no longer correctable
- You will not carry the emotional climate for them

When control cannot govern you, it stops trying to relate to you. It reallocates. It looks for a softer target. A new audience. A different supply line. The relationship doesn’t *end*. **It is discontinued.**

Why Some Losses Are Never Spoken of Again

Mutual relationships leave grief in the room. Control-based systems leave revision. When a system disappears, it often refuses narrative closure because closure requires honesty.

Honesty would require acknowledging harm, admitting pattern, admitting motive, admitting dependence, admitting loss. And those admissions threaten the identity that necessitated control.

So the system protects itself with a different move: it acts as if you never mattered. Not openly. Subtly. You are not discussed. You are not mourned. You are not “remembered” with accuracy. You are replaced.

And when you are mentioned, it is often in one of two forms:

- **erasure**: nothing happened, nothing mattered, no story exists

- **containment**: a small, tidy explanation that keeps them clean and keeps you dubious

Because some losses are never spoken of again for one reason: speaking would make the mechanism visible.

Sometimes the system grieves louder *after* you leave than it ever cared while you stayed—because your presence was structural, not relational. What is mourned is not you, but the loss of access, regulation, and control your presence provided.

Sometimes this loss manifests not as silence but as visible grief. Tears may appear. Fixation may linger. A sense of devastation may surface long after the relationship has ended. This does not contradict disappearance. It explains it. What is being mourned is not your interior life, your dignity, or your reality—but the collapse of a structure that depended on your presence to function. Control-based systems can grieve the loss of power without ever recognising the person who carried it. They can feel the destabilisation of authority while still refusing accountability, repair, or equality. This is not relational grief. It is ***structural loss*** registering in the body while the identity protects itself from truth. And because naming the real loss would expose the mechanism, the mourning remains unspoken, unresolved, and safely disconnected from you.

This kind of grief often looks intense because it is real—but it is real in a precise way. It is the body registering destabilisation while the psyche refuses meaning. It is sensation without insight, pain without reckoning, emotion without responsibility. What collapses is not attachment, but certainty. What breaks is not love, but the assumption of permanence.

Sometimes this grief is confused—even by the person experiencing it—for regret. But regret that arrives only after exit is not recognition; it is a miscalculation revealing itself too late. It is the shock of discovering that what was assumed to be permanent was, in fact, voluntary. The tears do not come from having seen you clearly. They come from realising that consequences have arrived without the possibility of reversal. This kind of regret does not move toward repair, because repair would require equality. It does not seek accountability, because accountability would require truth. Instead, it lingers as private sorrow—felt, but never integrated—because acknowledging what was actually lost would mean confronting how power was used, how narratives were shaped, and how certainty replaced care. What is mourned is not the harm done, but the mistaken belief that you would endure it forever.

This is why the grief can be so intense and yet so disconnected. ***It is not about you.*** It is about the end of access without consent, the end of certainty without reciprocity, the end of a system that mistook your endurance for entitlement. Because the loss is structural rather than relational, it cannot be healed by apology or reflection. It can only be endured—quietly, privately, and without transformation.

What disappears is not their feeling, but the system's ability to pretend it was love—because reckoning would require equality, and silence keeps it tidy.

The Signature Tell

Here is the tell that you are not dealing with heartbreak. You are dealing with a system shutting down.

You will notice:

- A sudden, total absence of curiosity
- No genuine attempt at repair
- No questions that suggest attachment to your inner life
- No confusion, only distance
- No sorrow, only shutdown

It can feel surreal because the person may appear calm. But *calm is not the same as care.* Sometimes, quiet is just what remains when the system no longer needs to perform.

What Their Disappearance Means

Disappearance is not peace. It is not growth. It is not respect. It is the most efficient outcome once you are no longer governable.

Because when you cannot be managed:

- Your presence becomes a risk
- Your clarity becomes a threat
- Your memory becomes evidence

So they vanish. And the vanishing is meant to do one last thing: make you doubt your own reality. Make you wonder if you "overreacted". Make you miss the version that tethered you. It makes you feel foolish for naming what was real.

But disappearance is not proof that you were wrong. **It is proof that you ended the conditions that made the structure profitable.**

The Clean Ending

This is the moment Part IV has been moving toward. Not the moment you win. *The moment the system cannot continue.*

When they don't retaliate—they disappear—what you are watching is not restraint. **It is collapse.** A system that cannot survive in daylight does not stay to be examined. It goes dark.

And the quiet it leaves behind is not emptiness. It is evidence.

This is not closure.
It is the end of influence.

You were not abandoned because you were unlovable. **You were removed because you were ungovernable.**

Rupture isn't the explosion. It's the moment the system stops working on you. The silence, the retreat, the disappearance—none of it is closure. It's the mechanism losing access. And once access is gone, the story can't be rewritten from the inside anymore.

What's left is not grief's drama, but **clarity's precision**: you see what happened, you see what it cost, and you stop calling survival *love*.

V

✦ AFTER CLARITY ✦

Life on the other side of illusion

Clarity doesn't always feel like relief.
Sometimes it feels like weight: memories you can't unlearn,
trust that can't return to innocence, losses without neat endings.
But clarity is also a border. It changes what reaches you,
who can stay close, what "calm" means now.

This is life after illusion—where peace is quiet, access is earned,
and freedom looks ordinary.
This book does not ask you to act.
It asks you to live from what you can now

✦ Losses That Are Carried, Not Healed ✦

Why some experiences don't "resolve" • Why memory becomes instruction

Some losses are not transitional.
They are not passages you move through on the way to something gentler.
They do not offer narrative comfort or emotional resolution.
They do not promise healing as an endpoint, nor do they reward endurance with closure.

These losses resist redemption. They refuse to be reframed as lessons neatly learned or pain neatly transformed.

They do not close. They do not arc toward forgiveness. They do not settle into meaning. They do not soften with time. They remain.

Not as wounds that bleed—but as weight that teaches you how to stand.

This is the kind of loss that does not demand your attention, because it has already claimed it. It does not ache loudly. It does not reopen. It simply stays, altering posture, pace, and proportion. You do not "get over" it. You adjust around it. You build strength in response to its presence. You learn where your balance is now.

They reorganise you.

Not by breaking you—but by making certain illusions impossible to carry. They strip away unnecessary movement. They clarify what can no longer be held lightly. They change the way you inhabit your body, your time, your relationships. They recalibrate your threshold for what matters and what no longer earns your energy.

These losses do not ask to be understood. They ask to be integrated.

And once they are, you are not the same person who was hurt—but you are no longer the person who could be hurt in the same way again.

Why Some Experiences Don't "Resolve"

Resolution assumes reciprocity. It assumes acknowledgement, remorse, repair, and shared reality. But many losses occur in the absence of all four. They come from systems that disappeared instead of answering. From dynamics that ended without truth. From bonds that extracted more than they ever named.

No conversation completes those stories—because the story was never mutual to begin with. So the psyche does something else. It stops seeking resolution and starts seeking orientation. Not *How do I feel better about this?* But *what did this teach me about danger, access, and cost?*

This is not avoidance. It is an adaptation. Some losses are carried because the nervous system does not file them as *past.* It files them as information. Some experiences cannot be healed because healing would require denying what they revealed.

The Myth of Closure

There is a reason the instruction to *"move on"* arrives so quickly, so reflexively, and so universally. It is rarely about your healing. It is about restoring comfort—often not yours, but everyone else's. Healing that requires learning, discernment, and structural awareness is inconvenient. It disrupts narratives. It refuses erasure. It makes harm legible.

The world will pressure you to "move on" because moving on makes other people comfortable. It quiets tension. It reassures those who benefit from amnesia. It allows life to continue without reckoning.

Closure is often imposed on the injured by systems that never intend to be accountable. It is framed as maturity, strength, or peace, but its function is compliance. It suggests that healing entails relinquishing memory rather than integrating it. It suggests that peace is something you owe the past, rather than something you build by learning from it.

This framing subtly reverses responsibility. The burden shifts from the structure that caused harm to the survivor. The problem is no longer what happened, but how long you are still affected by it.

But not all losses are the same.

But some losses cannot be closed because they were not accidents. They were patterns. They were structures. They were predictable. They unfolded exactly as designed. To close them neatly would require treating them as isolated events rather than systemic realities.

To *"resolve"* them emotionally would be to misname them. It would be to sanitise repetition. It would be to grant innocence where there was design.

So the mind refuses, not out of bitterness—but out of accuracy.

This refusal is not pathological. It is discernment. It is the psyche recognising that forgetting would not be healing—it would be dangerous. It would invite repetition. It would betray what was learned at cost.

Some losses do not ask to be soothed. They ask to be understood. And understanding, once reached, does not dissolve. It becomes part of how you move through the world—quietly, precisely, without apology.

Because there are experiences you do not *get over.*

You get **clear**.

And clarity is not something you abandon to make other people comfortable.

Why Memory Becomes Instruction

There comes a point where memory is no longer emotional. It is no longer searching for comfort, validation, or repair. It stops circling the past in the hope that something different might be felt this time. When repair is impossible, the memory changes its function. It becomes practical. It becomes organised. It becomes protective.

When repair is impossible, memory becomes functional. It stops replaying for catharsis and starts organising for protection. **Memory begins to say:** *Notice this. Don't minimise that. This is where the cost* *started. This is the signal you missed last time.*

This shift is often misunderstood. It is labelled as obsession, inability to forgive, or failure to let go. But this is not memory clinging to pain. It is memory refusing to allow repetition. It is the mind converting experience into guidance, because the price of innocence has already been paid.

This is not rumination. It is calibration. When a person is repeatedly pressured to retract their perception, the psyche adapts by splitting: one part survives by complying, the other keeps the record. One part learns how to stay. The other learns how to remember. This is not pathology. It is intelligence under constraint.

The moment retraction stops—even once—the split collapses. **Memory floods not because the person is stuck, but because reality is finally allowed to return.** What appears to be fixation is integration delayed by years of forced denial. The mind is not reliving the past; it is reclaiming continuity.

The body remembers tone. Timing. Patterns of withdrawal. The feel of conditional warmth. These are not details stored for drama. They are stored because they were once dismissed, overridden, or explained away. The nervous system catalogues what language was not allowed to hold.

And once memory becomes instructional, you stop trying to *"move on"* from it. You move *with* it. You no longer ask memory to quiet itself. You ask it what it knows.

Memory becomes instruction when the cost of forgetting is too high—

not because you're afraid, but because you're trained in truth.

At that point, memory is no longer about the past. It is about preventing the future from repeating itself.

Carrying Is Not Failing to Heal

There is a quiet cruelty in telling people they should have "healed by now"—as if insight has an expiration date, as if discernment is pathology, as if remembering accurately is the same as being stuck.

Carrying a loss does not mean you are trapped by it. It means you integrated the lesson. You no longer walk into the same rooms unprepared. You no longer confuse calm with safety. You no longer trade dignity for reassurance. What you carry is not pain. *It is orientation.*

Staying did not mean you were blind. It meant you were human inside a system that punished sight.

Often, clarity completes itself only after departure—when the system no longer tries to keep you, but tries to control the meaning of your leaving.

If, after endurance, repair attempts, and emotional exhaustion, you leave and are recast as disloyal, ungrateful, or incapable of commitment, the relationship was sustained by your tolerance, not by mutual care.
If choosing self-preservation is reframed as betrayal, the bond requires your self-sacrifice to survive.
If the story becomes that you "couldn't last" rather than that the system was untenable, accountability is being avoided through character assassination.

If the years you stayed are erased the moment you leave, loyalty was only valued while it served control.
If your departure is used as proof of your defect rather than as evidence of a broken structure, the relationship was never interested in truth—only compliance.
If peace is offered only after you disappear or diminish, your presence—not your behaviour—was the threat.

The Difference Between Scar and Compass

Not all pain has the same function. Some damage simply marks where something broke—other damage changes how you navigate the world. The difference matters.

A scar marks where damage occurred. A compass tells you where not to go again. A scar is evidence of injury; a compass is evidence of learning. A scar can ache—a compass orients. A scar remembers the past. A compass protects the future.

Some losses leave scars. Others give you a compass. The distinction is not about severity—it is about consequence. Scars speak to what was endured. Compasses speak to what was understood. One records harm; the other reorganises choice.

You don't revisit them for emotion. You reference them for direction. Not to feel again, not to relive, not to grieve endlessly—but to orient yourself with accuracy. The memory is no longer raw; it is precise.

They inform: **who gets access; how quickly trust is extended; which explanations you no longer entertain; which silences you no longer endure.** These are not walls. They are coordinates. They do not narrow your life—they keep it from repeating its most costly detours.

This is not bitterness. It is not avoidance. It is not a closing of the heart. **This is not hardness. It is intelligence earned at a cost.**

A compass does not argue with terrain. It simply tells the truth about direction. And once you have one, you stop asking whether you are being unkind for not returning. You understand that clarity is not cruelty—and that wisdom does not require permission.

Some experiences are not meant to soften you.

They are meant to orient you.

The Quiet Outcome

People often mistake this kind of clarity for heaviness. They read gravity as burden, seriousness as stagnation, discernment as emotional weight. But clarity is not what slows you down—it is what stops you from bleeding energy into what cannot hold you.

But carrying a loss that taught you how to protect yourself is lighter than repeating the same injury with hope. Hope without accuracy is exhausting. Hope that ignores the pattern is costly. Protection learned through loss does not weigh you down—it frees you from reliving what already proved unsustainable.

You are not unresolved. You are informed. There is a distinction between being unfinished and being sufficiently complete to proceed without self-betrayal. Resolution implies something ended cleanly. Information implies that something was understood truthfully. And truth does not always come with neat endings.

And informed people do not need closure from systems that could not afford honesty. They stop waiting for explanations that would require accountability. They stop seeking peace from structures that depended on their confusion. They recognise that some systems cannot offer closure because closure would expose what they were built on.

They walk forward with memory as guidance—not to stay in the past, but to stop recreating it. Memory becomes directional rather than adhesive. It does not pull you backwards; it keeps you from circling. It does not trap you in what happened; it protects you from returning to it under a different name.

That is not unfinished healing. That is integration.

Integration is when the lesson no longer hurts to remember, but would hurt to ignore. It is when experience ceases to demand attention and begins quietly to shape choice.

And it changes everything that comes next.

✦ Why Easier Relationships Feel Emptier ✦

Why governable dynamics feel calm • Why depth requires equality • Why comfort is not intimacy

Easier relationships are not always safer. They are often quieter because **less of you is required**. Less of your truth. Less of your complexity. Less of your capacity to affect what happens next. Ease can be achieved in many ways, but one of the most reliable is simply to reduce the person inside it.

After clarity, many people notice something unsettling. Relationships that once would have felt "*peaceful*" now feel hollow. Pleasant. Smooth. Undemanding. And strangely empty. There is no obvious harm. No visible conflict. No apparent reason to leave. And yet something essential is missing.

This is not because you have become difficult.
It is because you have become **precise**.

You can no longer confuse ease with **depth**. You can no longer mistake the absence of tension for the presence of intimacy. You can feel the difference between calm that comes from mutual presence and calm that comes from mutual *avoidance*.

Ease without engagement no longer soothes you. It registers as an absence.
Smoothness without responsiveness no longer reassures you. It feels inert.
Quiet without contact no longer feels safe. It feels empty.

Once clarity arrives, your nervous system recalibrates. It stops settling for relationships that function only when you are reduced. It begins to require resonance, not just relief. Contact, not just calm.

And that shift is irreversible.

Because once you know what depth feels like—once you know what it means to be met rather than managed—you cannot unlearn the difference.

You do not become harder to love.
You become **less willing to disappear**.

And that changes what "easy" can ever mean again.

Why Governable Dynamics Feel Calm

Governable relationships are calm **by design**. Not because they are healthy, but because they are efficient. They minimise friction by minimising **you**—your range, your unpredictability, your capacity to disrupt the arrangement simply by being fully human.

The relationship runs smoothly because it has learned a single rule: **do not introduce complexity**. Complexity here does not mean chaos. It means a difference. It means dissent. It means need. It means a reality that cannot be pre-managed.

In these dynamics, there are fewer disagreements because your disagreement is not expected; fewer ruptures because your rupture is not accommodated; fewer negotiations because outcomes are already decided. What looks like harmony is often just the absence of permission.

The calm comes from **predictability**. You know what is acceptable, you know what will be rewarded, and you know what will quietly cost you. You learn the boundaries not through conversation, but through consequence. Over time, you stop testing them.

Nothing is contested.
Nothing is at risk.
Nothing truly moves.

This is why governable dynamics often feel *"easy"* at first. There is little tension because there is little **mutuality**. There is no friction because there is no real meeting of equals. You are not being met—you are being **managed**, gently enough that it doesn't hurt, carefully enough that it doesn't alarm.

But calm achieved through **asymmetry** is not peace.

It is **sedation**.

Sedation keeps the system stable by dulling sensation. It quiets discomfort without addressing the cause. It feels soothing until you realise it has cost you your movement, your voice, and your agency.

Peace can tolerate aliveness.

Sedation cannot.

And the moment you begin to wake up inside a governable calm, the system will no longer feel so gentle—because calm was never the goal.

Control was.

Why Depth Requires Equality

Depth only exists where two people can **affect each other**. Not observe each other. Not manage each other. Not coexist in parallel lanes—but *affect*. To affect is to have a consequence. To be able to land in someone else's interior world and be landed in, in return.

Equality introduces **risk**. It introduces the possibility that your truth might matter; that their discomfort might not end the conversation; that neither of you can fully control the outcome. There is no guaranteed safety in advance. No pre-agreed hierarchy that decides whose reality prevails.

This creates **tension**—not dysfunction, but *aliveness*. The tension of two autonomous people sharing space without one being required to shrink so the other can remain comfortable.

In equal relationships, there is negotiation rather than assumption, repair rather than erasure, accountability rather than performance, and change rather than compliance. These are not stylistic differences. They are structural ones. They determine whether a relationship can respond to reality—or must defend itself against it.

This kind of connection is not always smooth. It cannot be. It requires

presence, **responsiveness**, and the willingness to be altered by another human being. It requires tolerating influence without interpreting it as a threat.

That alteration is the point.

Depth is what happens when neither person is safely above the consequences of their actions, when no one is insulated from impact, when power does not protect one person from having to listen.

Depth is not comfort.
Depth is contact.

And contact only exists where equality is allowed to remain intact.

Why Comfort Is Not Intimacy

Comfort is often mistaken for **closeness**. It feels soothing. It feels familiar. It feels safe enough to stay. Comfort says: *nothing will be challenged; nothing will be asked too much; nothing will disturb the arrangement.* It offers predictability, ease, and a quiet promise that no one will press where it hurts.

Intimacy says something else. It says: *you can be seen without shrinking; you can be disagreed with without being punished; you can change without being abandoned.* Intimacy allows friction without rupture. It allows truth without threat. It does not require you to stay the same to stay connected.

Comfort protects the **system**.
Intimacy exposes it.

Comfort asks, "*Can we keep this pleasant?*"
Intimacy asks: *Can we stay true?*

Comfort prioritises stability. It smooths edges. It avoids tension. It preserves the existing shape of things. Intimacy tolerates uncertainty. It allows discomfort in the service of honesty. It accepts that closeness sometimes requires recalibration, not preservation.

This is why some relationships feel good but don't grow. They provide relief without resonance. **Stability without significance. Warmth without contact.** The surface feels kind. The atmosphere feels calm. But nothing essential is touched.

You are comfortable—but **not known**.

And being known is the risk intimacy takes that comfort never will.

The Shift That Makes Ease Feel Empty

After clarity, your nervous system stops settling for environments where your presence does not alter the room, your truth is tolerated but not engaged, and your needs are accommodated but not shared. What once felt "fine" begins to feel thin. What once passed as peace begins to register as absence. **You start to feel the lack of reciprocity as absence, not peace.** Not as drama, not as conflict, but as a quiet recognition that something essential is missing.

This is not restlessness. It is discernment. It is the internal recalibration that happens when your system has learned the difference between being included and being encountered, between being allowed and being met.

Your body now recognises the difference between calm that comes from safety and calm that comes from suppression. One expands you. The other keeps you manageable. One allows movement, voice, and change. The other depends on your containment. And once your body knows the difference, it will not mistake stillness for intimacy again.

Why This Can Feel Like Loss

There is often a quiet grief here—not for the relationship itself, but for the illusion that ease meant love. You may miss the simplicity, the lack of friction, the predictability. You may miss how uncomplicated it felt to stay when nothing was being asked of you beyond consistency and compliance. **But you no longer mistake those things for intimacy.**

You know now: **ease without equality is containment; harmony without voice is compliance; comfort without depth is emptiness with good lighting.** These are not metaphors; they are distinctions your body has learned to make. And once learned, they cannot be unlearned.

This is not dissatisfaction. It is accuracy. Accuracy that costs illusion. Accuracy that ends confusion. Accuracy that makes certain kinds of "easy" impossible to return to, because you can now feel the difference between being calm because you are safe and being calm because nothing of you is allowed to move.

The New Metric

After clarity, relationships are no longer measured by how easy they are to maintain, but by how real you are allowed to be inside them. Ease, once mistaken for success, is no longer persuasive on its own. Smoothness no longer signals safety by default. What matters now is not how little effort something requires, but how much of you it can hold without distortion.

The question shifts from *Does this feel calm?*—because calm can come from safety or from compliance—to ***Does this require my full humanity?*** Does it make room for your complexity, your changeability, your needs, your no? Does it allow you to arrive without editing, softening, or shrinking? Does it respond to your reality rather than merely tolerating it?

If the answer is no, the ease will eventually feel empty. It will feel hollow rather than restful, thin rather than peaceful. Not because something is missing from you—but because **something essential is missing from the relationship.** Something relational has been replaced by something functional. And once you are clear, you can no longer confuse comfort with contact, or maintenance with intimacy.

What This Prepares You For

This chapter is not teaching you to seek struggle. It is teaching you to stop mistaking the absence of resistance for connection—to stop reading smoothness as intimacy and quiet as proof of safety. It is teaching you to recognise that ease can be produced by accommodation just as easily as by care, and that not all calm is relational. Some calm is simply the result of you staying within acceptable limits.

Because ***depth is not loud—but it is alive.*** It carries movement, response, and consequence. It has texture. It changes you and allows itself to be changed in return. Depth contains friction without punishment, difference without withdrawal, truth without collapse. It does not require constant intensity—but it does require equality.

And once you know what aliveness feels like—once your body recognises the difference between being met and being managed—ease without equality can no longer satisfy you. It does not offend you. It does not alarm you. It simply fails to register as nourishment.

It simply passes through. Quietly. Unmistakably. ***Empty.***

Because clarity does not make you restless, it makes you accurate. And accuracy cannot be soothed by what only ever worked when you were smaller.

✦ Who Can Access You Now ✦

How discernment changes proximity · Why some people self-select out · Why boundaries do the filtering

Clarity does not make you guarded. It makes you precise. Precision is not defence; it is discernment refined by reality. Guardedness comes from fear. Precision comes from understanding. Fear closes. Understanding clarifies. After the illusion collapses, you no longer relate from instinct alone. You relate from sight—from pattern recognised, consequence tracked, and cost remembered.

After illusion collapses, access is no longer granted by familiarity, history, chemistry, or need. Those once felt sufficient because they were unexamined. Familiarity felt like safety. history felt like obligation. Chemistry felt like the truth. Need felt like purpose. They carried emotional weight, but no structural guarantee. Illusion taught you—slowly, painfully—that none of these ensures mutuality. None of these protects dignity. None of these guarantees care when pressure arrives.

It is granted by alignment. Alignment of values. Alignment of accountability. Alignment of how power is held, how care is given, and how reality is faced when things are uncomfortable. Alignment is not loud.

It does not rush intimacy. It does not mistake intensity for truth. It reveals itself over time through consistency, not urgency; through behaviour under strain, not declarations made in ease.

You stop treating proximity as proof of love, and that single shift changes everything about who remains close. Presence must now earn its place. Access must now justify itself. Closeness without integrity no longer persuades you. Intensity without alignment no longer binds you. What once felt magnetic but destabilising loses its authority.

Not because you became harder—because you became accurate.

Accuracy removes what was never meant to stay. It filters without cruelty. It clarifies without apology. It does not punish—it simply refuses distortion. And what remains is not smaller. **It is truer.**

How Discernment Changes Proximity

Discernment is not suspicion. It is pattern recognition without negotiation. It does not scan for threats; it recognises structure. It does not assume harm; it remembers evidence. Discernment does not interrogate intent—it tracks consequence. It watches what repeats, what costs you, and what requires you to shrink to continue. It listens to the body, the aftermath, the residue left behind after contact.

After clarity, you stop asking, "Do they like me?" That question belonged to uncertainty. It belonged to the hope that approval could substitute for safety, that being wanted could compensate for being diminished. You start asking, "Do they respect my reality?" Because respect does not fluctuate with mood. It does not evaporate under pressure. It does not require persuasion. Respect remains intact even when agreement does not.

Proximity reorganises itself around new criteria: who responds to your no without penalty; who does not require you to explain your limits; who does not grow colder when you become clearer; who does not benefit from your confusion; who remains steady when you stop over-giving. These are not preferences. They are diagnostics. They tell you who can remain close without eroding you.

What once felt like a connection but required constant management no longer qualifies as such. What once felt intense but depended on your silence no longer holds weight. You are no longer measuring closeness by chemistry, familiarity, or shared history—but by impact, consistency, and the absence of punishment.

Discernment shortens the distance between you and what is real—and widens the distance between you and what only functioned when you were pliable. It collapses the illusion quickly. It does not linger where truth has already spoken.

This is not a withdrawal. **It is calibration.**

Why Some People Self-Select Out

You will not need to push many people away. They leave on their own. This is one of the quiet truths clarity reveals: separation does not always require force. It often occurs naturally, as a consequence of reality becoming less negotiable. When you stop cushioning discomfort, translating behaviour, smoothing tension, offering unlimited access, and making yourself smaller to preserve harmony, some people experience your clarity as rejection. **Not because you rejected them, but because**

you removed the role they were using you for. What disappears is not the relationship, but the function you were quietly fulfilling inside it.

People who required your emotional labour, your silence, your flexibility, your forgiveness without repair, your availability without reciprocity cannot remain once those are no longer on offer. These dynamics do not end with confrontation; they end with incompatibility. So they drift. They disengage. They vanish. **Not because you changed—because the conditions changed.** When access is no longer unconditional, those who depended on that condition quietly lose interest.

Why Boundaries Do the Filtering

Boundaries do not test people. They reveal them. They reveal who was only there because you had none. This is why boundaries feel so decisive: they collapse ambiguity. They remove the need for interpretation and allow behaviour to speak for itself.

A boundary is not a demand. It is information. And information clarifies who can stay. Those who respond with curiosity, respect, adjustment, and steadiness remain. Those who respond with pressure, guilt, withdrawal, mockery, or escalation remove themselves. The boundary does not eject them; **their response to it does.**

This is why boundaries feel lonely at first. They end access faster than they create intimacy. They reduce noise before they produce depth. But over time, they yield something rarer and more stable: **relationships that do not require defence.** Relationships where your presence does not need to be protected because it is not being exploited.

The New Shape of Closeness

After clarity, closeness becomes quieter. There is less intensity, less urgency, less emotional theatre—and more consistency, accountability, ease without erasure, connection that does not cost you. The absence of volatility is not a loss of passion; it is the presence of safety.

You are no longer surrounded by many people. You are accompanied by the right ones. And the difference is felt in the body: **you do not brace; you do not perform; you do not prepare for consequence. You arrive as you are—and nothing in the room tightens in response.** There is no penalty for honesty, no withdrawal for autonomy.

The Cost—and the Return

Yes, fewer people have access to you now. That is not a failure of openness. It is the result of accuracy. You did not lose connection. You lost distortion. And what remains may be smaller—but it is real. **It is reciprocal. It is stable without being static.** It does not depend on your confusion to survive, and it does not require you to disappear to stay.

What clarity takes away in quantity, it returns in integrity. And integrity, once restored, changes the entire architecture of closeness.

What This Chapter Leaves You With

What this chapter leaves you with is not instruction, but orientation. Not rules, but a recalibration of how closeness, access, and belonging actually work once illusion has fallen away.

Access is no longer earned by need, persistence, or familiarity. Those currencies once felt persuasive because they were emotionally charged: need evoked responsibility, persistence mimicked devotion, and familiarity masqueraded as safety. But clarity reveals their limits. **It is earned by respect for your clarity, tolerance for your autonomy, and willingness to meet you without hierarchy.** Not symbolic respect, not conditional tolerance, not rhetorical equality—but lived, repeatable behaviour that holds steady when power could be abused and isn't.

Everyone else will feel your boundaries as distance—not because you are withholding, but because they were never meant to come this close. Some people were only able to approach you through confusion, overfunctioning, or your willingness to accommodate imbalance. When that doorway closes, what they experience is not loss of you, but loss of access. **And once you accept that, proximity stops being confusing. It becomes clean.** You no longer have to decode who is near you for connection and who is near you for convenience. Distance stops feeling like rejection and begins to feel like accuracy.

In the final chapter, we name what this creates—not excitement, not triumph, not drama—but the quiet shape of freedom. Not freedom as escape or victory, but freedom as the absence of distortion. The freedom of no longer needing to negotiate your worth, explain your limits, or justify your clarity. The freedom of a life organised around what is real, not what once demanded your doubt.

This is not an ending that announces itself. It is one that settles—and stays.

✦ The Quiet Shape of Freedom ✦

Why freedom is undramatic • Why safety feels ordinary • Why peace doesn't announce itself

Freedom does not arrive like a breakthrough. It arrives like the absence of a task. No more scanning tone. No more rehearsing sentences. No more managing timing. No more bracing for consequences. What disappears first is not pain, but vigilance—the constant readiness that once kept you safe by keeping you small. At first, it can feel empty—because your nervous system was busy for so long that stillness reads as missing. But nothing is missing. **The system is.**

Why Freedom Is Undramatic

Freedom is not a performance. It is not revenge. It is not closure. It is the end of negotiation with what was never mutual. It does not need witnesses because it is not proving anything. It is not correcting the past. It is simply no longer organised around it.

Freedom looks like: making a decision and not defending it; leaving a message unanswered and not translating your silence; saying no and not staying to soothe the reaction; choosing yourself without building a case for why you're allowed. These acts look small from the outside. Internally, they represent the collapse of an entire structure that depended on your participation.

In the old structure, everything required effort: clarity, boundaries, reality itself. You had to carry truth uphill. You had to earn neutrality. You had to manage consequences that were never yours to hold. In freedom, effort drops away. Not because life becomes easy—but because your life is no longer organised around managing someone else's access to you. The labour ends. The vigilance stands down.

This is why freedom is quiet. There is no audience. No argument to win. No story to prove. **Just the return of your time to you.**

Why Safety Feels Ordinary

People expect safety to feel like intensity. Like certainty. Like someone insisting they'll never leave. That expectation itself is learned under pressure—learned in environments where unpredictability was paired with attachment, where relief followed anxiety, where being chosen required vigilance. But real safety does not spike your nervous system. **It doesn't need to.**

Safety feels ordinary because it doesn't demand constant monitoring. It does not require you to scan tone, interpret pauses, or manage reactions in advance. In safety: **your no is accepted the first time; your boundaries don't create punishment; disagreement doesn't become a threat; your body doesn't tighten when you speak; affection doesn't become a bargaining chip.** Nothing needs to be managed because nothing is being extracted. Your presence is not being evaluated for usefulness. Your compliance is not the price of connection.

Nothing dramatic happens because nothing has to. There is no emotional tax to pay to remain included. **You are not rewarded for shrinking. You are not punished for existing. You don't have to earn the right to be fully real.** That absence of performance can feel unfamiliar at first—almost flat—because your nervous system was trained to associate love with activation, closeness with consequence.

That is why safety can feel almost disappointing at first. It does not arrive with fireworks or urgency. It does not feel like chemistry engineered by tension. **It doesn't feel like chemistry. It feels like a room.**

Why Peace Doesn't Announce Itself

Peace does not enter with declarations. It does not require a witness. It is recognised in the most minor, most telling details: you sleep without replaying; you speak without preparing; you walk into a room without calculating; you leave without panic; you stop needing to be understood by people committed to misunderstanding you.

Peace is not a high. It is the absence of extraction. Freedom is not the absence of pain. **It is the absence of distortion.** What is gone is not feeling, but contortion—the constant reshaping of yourself to fit a structure that never fit you.

And because it doesn't come with fireworks, many people miss it at first. They look for the familiar markers—intensity, urgency, the feeling of being needed. But being needed is not the same as being safe. A system needs you. **Freedom does not.** Freedom lets you be optional without being erased.

The Quiet Proof

There is a moment—often so understated it could be missed—when you notice you are no longer organising your life around someone else's reactions. This moment does not arrive as triumph or relief. It arrives as completion. Not because you are numb—**because you are finished**. Finished negotiating reality. Finished auditing your tone. Finished wondering if you were fair enough. Finished living as though your legitimacy depended on someone else's interpretation.

You stop checking if you should have explained better. You stop bargaining with memory, stop reopening scenes that were already resolved in the body long before the mind caught up. You still remember. Memory does not vanish. But it no longer governs you. **You simply don't live inside it.**

This is the quiet shape of freedom: you are not constantly returning to the scene—mentally, emotionally, or relationally. You are no longer rehearsing, recalibrating, or preparing for impact. **You are no longer available to it.** Not because you are hardened or avoidant, but because your nervous system has concluded the negotiation. The loop has closed.

And what remains is not emptiness. It is space—space where vigilance used to live, space where self-doubt once laboured, space where your life can finally move forward without reference to what no longer holds authority over you.

What This Chapter Leaves You With

Freedom is not loud. It does not announce itself as victory. It is a life where your dignity is not up for debate; your nervous system is not a negotiation table; your clarity is not punished; your boundaries do not create drama—only distance.

You don't feel powerful every day. You feel ordinary. And for someone who has lived inside control, **that ordinary is the miracle**: no performance, no bracing, no need to disappear.

Just you—**unmanaged, ungovernable, and finally unassigned.**

Epilogue

What You Knew Before You Could Say It

Before there were words, there was knowing. Not the kind you could argue for. Not the kind you could prove. The kind that lived in your body before your mind learned how to explain it away.

You felt it as a tightening. A pause. A subtle withdrawal of trust that happened before you could justify it. You noticed when the warmth changed temperature, when silence stopped feeling spacious and started feeling strategic, when care began to cost you something unnamed.

You knew before you understood.

And because you could not yet say it, you learned to manage it. To soften it. To doubt it. To translate it into something more acceptable.

This book was never meant to give you new instincts. It was meant to return you to the ones you were trained to override. Nothing here was meant to convince you. *Convincing belongs to systems that need your doubt.* This was meant to organise what you already sensed but were discouraged from trusting.

That the body notices before the mind agrees.

That calm is not always safety.
That explanation is not the same as clarity.
That some silences are rehearsals.
That fairness can provoke rage.
That refusal is not cruelty.
That disappearance is not indifference.
That freedom is quiet.

You were not wrong for feeling unsettled before anything "happened." You were not dramatic for noticing patterns before they were undeniable. You were not broken for carrying what never resolved.

You were responding to structure.

And once you can see structure, you cannot unsee it. Not because you become suspicious—but because you become *precise.*

The ending of this book is not a transformation. It is a return to the moment when your body leaned back slightly, and your mind rushed forward to compensate. To the feeling you explained away because you did not yet have language, to the clarity that arrived long before permission did.

Nothing here asks you to confront. Nothing asks you to expose. Nothing asks you to perform strength. It asks you to stop cooperating with distortion. To trust that if something requires your confusion, it is not for you. That if something collapses when you become clear, it was never stable. That if peace feels ordinary, it is because it finally belongs to you.

You do not need to announce what you see now. You do not need to justify how you move. You do not need to make meaning for anyone else. Your life will reorganise quietly around what no longer costs you.

And one day—without ceremony—you will realise: you are not explaining. You are not bracing. You are not waiting for the snap shut. You are simply living inside what you knew all along.

That is not awakening. *It is alignment*—and it does not negotiate.

About the Author

Miriam Mathew writes at the intersection of perception and power—where people sense something is wrong long before they can articulate why. Her work is concerned less with events than with structures: how systems operate, how clarity is delayed, and how the body registers truth before language can catch up.

Across her writing, she returns to the same questions:
What happens when calm is not safety?
What collapses when patterns are named?
And why does clarity so often arrive quietly, without witnesses?

She is the author of several books and brings a lifelong attention to patterns, systems, and the cost of misnaming what is happening. Her work does not ask readers to act, confront, or explain—but to trust what they have already noticed and allow their lives to reorganise around that accuracy.

Connect with the Author

This book was written for people who learned to doubt themselves in environments that required confusion to function.

If these pages resonated, it is likely because they did not introduce something new, but named something you already knew and were discouraged from trusting. This work is not about confrontation or performance. It is about clarity, self-possession, and the quiet return of agency.

My work centres on helping people recognise patterns of control, coercion, and misalignment—especially those that hide behind care, commitment, or respectability. Through writing, teaching, and reflection, I explore how clarity restores dignity, how discernment protects life, and how freedom often arrives without drama.

If this book helped you name something accurately, you are welcome to continue the conversation in the spaces below. There is no expectation to explain yourself, prove your experience, or provide insight. Clarity speaks for itself.

Stay Connected

Website:
redefineyournarrative.com

Email:
redefineyournarrative@gmail.com | connectwithmiriam@redefineyou rnarrative.com

Instagram:
@redefineyournarrative

Additional writings, reflections, and future projects are shared through these channels.

Thank you for reading with attention and honesty.
Nothing here asks you to become louder—only more exact.

Also by Miriam Mathew

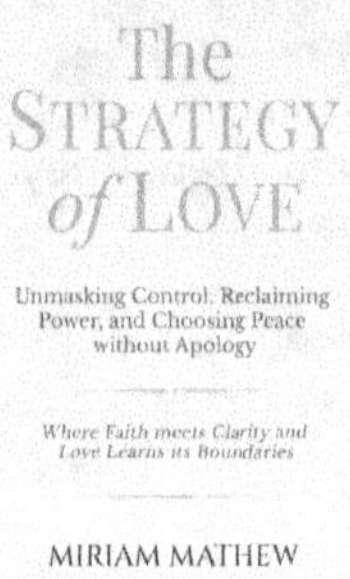

The Strategy of Love

The Strategy of Love is a lived examination of discernment over time—how the body tracks tone, body language, trajectory, and cost long before language arrives. It follows the subtle early signals that are often dismissed as "overthinking" and shows how clarity emerges through observation, patience, and pattern recognition rather than confrontation. It is a book about unmasking control, reclaiming power, and choosing peace without apology.

www.ingramcontent.com/pod-product-compliance
Lightning Source LLC
LaVergne TN
LVHW020042110826
845155LV00029B/605

* 9 7 8 1 9 1 9 4 4 1 7 1 9 *